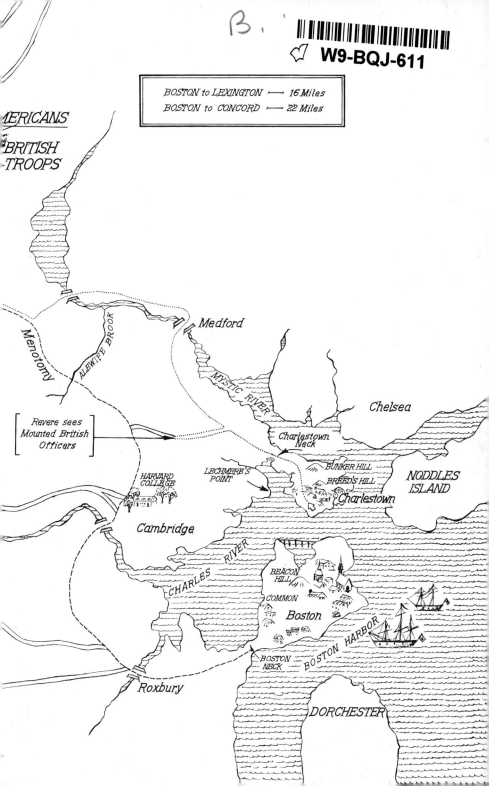

$\mathcal{B}.$

W9-BQJ-611

BOSTON to LEXINGTON ⟶ 16 Miles
BOSTON to CONCORD ⟶ 22 Miles

AMERICANS

BRITISH
TROOPS

Menotomy

ALEWIFE BROOK

Medford

MYSTIC RIVER

Chelsea

Charlestown
Neck

[ Revere sees
Mounted British
Officers ]

HARVARD
COLLEGE

LECHMERE'S
POINT

BUNKER HILL

BREED'S HILL

NODDLES
ISLAND

Charlestown

Cambridge

CHARLES RIVER

BEACON
HILL

COMMON

Boston

BOSTON
NECK

BOSTON HARBOR

Roxbury

DORCHESTER

# THE
# SIEGE OF
# BOSTON

By the Same Author

# HISTORICAL

Goodbye to Gunpowder

The Birth of the Constitution
*An Informal History*

July 4, 1776

Valley Forge

The Battle of New Orleans
*An Informal History of the War
That Nobody Wanted: 1812*

Victory at Yorktown

The Great Separation
*The Story of the Boston Tea Party and the
Beginning of the American Revolution*

The Tide Turns
*An Informal History of the Campaign
of 1776 in the American Revolution*

# BIOGRAPHY

Elizabeth I

John the Great
*The Times and Life of John L. Sullivan*

The Gentleman from New York
*A Biography of Roscoe Conkling*

Sir Humphrey Gilbert

Sir Walter Raleigh

Marlborough
*The Portrait of a Conqueror*

Bonnie Prince Charlie

Knolly and Mary
from Don Chidsey
Aloha!

# THE
# SIEGE OF
# BOSTON

*An on-the-scene account*
*of the beginning*
*of the American Revolution*

## Donald Barr Chidsey

CROWN PUBLISHERS, INC., NEW YORK

*All pictures courtesy New York Public Library Picture Collection*

# CONTENTS

To *Alan Clark Chidsey*

# 1

Boston was in a state of intolerable strain, while the hinterland scintillated with rumors. Something, everybody knew, was about to explode.

It was a day of diaries, and a brash young lieutenant of the King's Own wrote into his, April 15, 1775: "Genl. Orders. 'The Grenadiers and Light Infantry in order to learn Grenadrs. Exercise and new evolutions are to be off all duties 'till further orders.' This I suppose is by way of a blind. I dare say they have something for them to do."[1]

He was right; but he was not alone. For many months the troops cooped in Boston had been doing nothing but snarling at the civilians, who snarled back. It was common knowledge that Lieutenant General Thomas Gage— "Tommy" to the rank and file, in the officers' messes "The Old Woman"—had lately received from the War Office a letter telling him to get busy. As governor of Massachusetts and commander-in-chief of all the British forces in America, he was sitting on a powder keg, there in the closed port of Boston. The provincials, the self-styled patriots, had set up a congress of their own, which was, surely, an illegal body, but which nevertheless seemed to work. They were openly preparing for combat, assembling supplies at key points, reorganizing their militia, keeping in touch with events in the capital by means of dispatch riders. They must be awed by a show of might. Gage was a kindly man, a cautious man—"mild," his own sovereign called him—and he shuddered at the thought of open battle, often messy, always expensive. He had been

GENERAL THOMAS GAGE

residing among the Americans for many years, and he liked them; he was married to one, a New Jersey girl. He hoped to retire quietly, soon. The last thing he wanted was a war.

Gage did not get along well with his naval opposite number at Boston, a bumptious admiral named Graves—their wives couldn't stand each other—so that when that curious order went out to the light infantry and the grenadiers, and at the same time there was an unprecedented example of co-operation between the army and the navy, folks smelled a rat. At the request of the general all the boats in the naval vessels in Boston harbor were overhauled, stocked with oars, and put into the water.

It is not likely, however, that many persons surmised that it was something that would shake the world.

There was nothing new about the discontentment on

both sides, which had existed since the end of the French and Indian War twelve years ago; but it was worse than ever, and growing still worse all the time. Gage would have to act, and seemingly he was about to. Where would the blow fall?

The French and Indian War—known to Europeans as the Seven Years' War—had ended with the Peace of Paris, which took Canada from France and handed it to Great Britain. That war had been expensive. The victor, at its close, was at once the richest nation in the world and the deepest in debt, as taxes showed. Why should not the American colonies pay some of those taxes? The colonists were protected by the British Army, weren't they? Then why should they not be expected in part at least to support that army?

The colonists did not agree. They could not abide being taxed by somebody three thousand miles away, somebody, moreover, in whose appointment or election they had been granted no voice, and over whose decisions they had no control. As for protection, *what* protection? Now that there was no longer a French army in Canada ready at any time to sweep down upon New England, New York, or Pennsylvania, what had the middle and northern colonies to fear? Without the French to goad them, the Indians were unlikely to make any serious raids. Anyway, the Indians were far away from the prosperous towns of the coast. The frontiersmen could take care of the Indians. Redcoats were not needed for a job like that.

Nevertheless, redcoats were sent, and taxes were imposed, and feelings ran high, so that a clash became, it seemed, inevitable.

The Molasses Act, the sugar acts, the stamp riots, the Boston Massacre, the Tea Party, and now this—this order for a hushed gathering of crack troops at night.

Oh, decidedly something was up!

Two gay young British officers, "disguised as countrymen, in brown cloaths and reddish handkerchiefs round our necks,"[2] had recently ambled through the nearby villages and towns, sketching as they went. They had been recognized as spies everywhere, and it was duly reported to the Provincial Congress that they had shown the most interest in and asked the most questions about Concord, slightly less than twenty miles from Boston. It was at Concord that the Congress had established its largest supply of gunpowder, flour, lead, and other warlike materials.

There was no difficulty in drawing a conclusion.

Boston was a pear-shaped peninsula attached to the mainland only by its "stem," the Neck, in the south. All the rest was bordered by water. The Neck was only a few yards across, and once it was fortified—two 24-pounders, eight 9-pounders, breastworks—and once all boats had been seized, it was easy to confine the Bostonians. As things in town grew taut, then, the leaders of the independence party got out. There was one notable exception.

Dr. Joseph Warren was a slim, handsome, eager-eyed man of thirty-three, an outstanding social success with a remunerative practice. He had a fondness for showy clothes, especially for glittering gold-thread or silver-thread waistcoats. He had a fondness, too, for his country, and he was in the thickest of what General Gage classed as a conspiracy. All the same, he stayed in Boston. He might expect a rap on the door of his house in Hanover Street any midnight now; but he stayed.

He had assistance, patriots of somewhat lesser station but equal ardor, and notably that talented silversmith and dentist Paul Revere, who, though he was middle-aged, and overweight to boot, was a tireless horseman. April 7, Warren had sent Revere to Concord with a warning that in Boston it looked like action soon. Gage had been informed of this visit by one of his spies.

Matters came to a head the night of April 18. It was a Tuesday.

CHAPTER

2

THAT grenadiers and light infantrymen were to be used was significant. The practice of making up a task force from these two classes, taken out of sundry regiments, was still a new one in the British Army. There were many who still believed that although the light infantry and the grenadiers were the best in the ranks, the cream of the crop, it was poor policy to break up the traditional grouping by regiments. Thomas Gage was not such a believer, and that he resorted to this new and somewhat daring device was in itself significant.

There were about 4,000 redcoats in Boston, a town ordinarily inhabited by about 15,000 civilians, though the latter had been much reduced because of the near-war situation. There were ten infantry regiments, several companies of marines, a few small artillery units, no cavalry, not even dragoons.

These men were touchy, their nerves frayed by long confinement in a city they disliked, among a people they despised—and distrusted. They were as edgy as race horses.

A British infantry regiment, on paper, consisted of 457 persons, a figure that included officers, both commissioned and noncommissioned, as well as the rank and file, but not drummers, fifers, surgeons, or camp followers. However, precious few of the regiments were anywhere near their full authorized strength. Recruiting had lagged, for even in Ireland, the lushest pasture of all, there was at that time, *mirabile dictu*, enough potatoes. The jails had been scraped;

but they had often been scraped before, and they yielded little. In addition, each regiment had some—the number might be as high as twenty—of what were called "contingent soldiers," imaginary men, whose pay, which was *not* imaginary, went into a regimental fund for widows and the wounded. Then too, there was sickness; and 15 percent on the sick list at any given time was considered good. Also, one and sometimes two of the ten regiments were stationed in Fort William, an island out in the bay.

Each regiment contained two elite companies, the grenadiers and the light infantry, which were called flank companies because when the regiment was drawn up in parade formation they closed the two ends of the line, and also because the light infantry at least, and sometimes the grenadiers as well, were often in fact employed in flank work when the regiment was advancing under fire or expected to be fired upon, they being especially trained for that sort of work. The light infantry were the *nimblest* men in the army. The grenadiers were, by and large, the *tallest*, many of them being picked with their height in mind; and in addition they wore a distinctive steeplelike hat that was calculated to make them look even bigger than they were. The grenadiers no longer carried grenades.

The light infantrymen and grenadiers at Boston, together with a company of marines told off to assist them, on the night of April 18–19 numbered between 600 and 700. They gathered with the greatest of stealth, like conspirators. Lieutenant Colonel Francis Smith, a fat, very slow man, was put in charge. His second-in-command was Major John Pitcairn, a middle-aged, red-faced Scot, of the marines.

Dr. Warren in Hanover Street knew all this as soon as it happened, though extraordinary precautions were taken in assembling the men and marching them to the Common, the sergeants awakening them with hands over their mouths and taking them out of the barracks by means of back doors.

WILLIAM DAWES, JR.

At about nine o'clock Dr. Warren got hold of one William Dawes, Jr., a volunteer dispatch rider, a husky man just turned thirty. Dawes had no love of redcoats, one of whom had lately made a pass at his, Dawes', wife. (Dawes beat the cad to a pulp, and was not punished for this, perhaps because the military were leaning over backward to avoid offending the touchy civilians, or perhaps because in this case the provocation was so pronounced.) Dawes was to ride to Concord and raise the alarm. He was to go by land, over the Neck. The Neck would be guarded, but Dawes had made it a point to know the guards personally: they would do almost anything for a little liquor. He had no trouble getting over.

It was an hour later, about ten o'clock, when Revere faced Dr. Warren. It is always safest to send two men two separate ways. Did the silversmith, a resourceful character, have a boat? Well, he knew where he could get one. Good; then he was to proceed, with the caution of a cat, across the

Charles River to the village and peninsula of Charlestown. Friends would be waiting for him there with a horse, for they would have been warned by lanterns hung in the steeple of the Old North Church that the redcoats were coming by water: this seemed certain now. Revere made off, two friends helping him.[3]

It was only a matter of less than half a mile, but the night was bright, the tides could be tricky, and it was necessary to pass almost under the counter of the great man-of-war *Somerset*, where an extra-sharp watch would be kept that night. "It was then young flood, the ship was winding, and the moon was rising."[4] In short, it was a touch-and-go operations; but they made it, and were met on the shore by William Conant, who had procured "a very good horse" from Deacon John Larkin of Charlestown.

Revere was warned that there were many riders on the Middlesex County roads that night, hard-bitten young British officers and their hard-bitten sergeants sent over the Neck for the purpose of intercepting just such messengers as Revere and Dawes. Richard Devins, of Charlestown, a member of the Committee of Safety, the action group of the Provincial Congress, had seen no fewer than ten of them on his way back from Watertown, where the committee had been meeting.

Revere was soon to learn the truth of this. He went northwest out of the Charlestown Peninsula, and where the Mystick lapped the road on his right he swung sharply to the left. This route, a lonesome one, would take him to Cambridge, where he could come out on the Brookline-Cambridge-Menotomy road,[5] his shortest way to Lexington and Concord. At or near Cambridge, too, he might meet up with Dawes, *if* Dawes had got through.

Revere never did get to Cambridge. There were two horsemen ahead of him, motionless under a tree. He could see from the cockades in their hats that they were officers. They

PAUL REVERE'S RIDE

hailed him. Revere was not armed; and anyway, it was not his part to play the hero, only to carry the news. He wheeled about and galloped back toward the Charlestown-Medford road. The officers pursued, but Deacon Larkin's horse shook them off.

Now Revere began to knock on doors, spreading the alarm.

Meanwhile something, as so often happens in the army, had gone wrong. The redcoats, acting according to orders, had proceeded virtually on tiptoe from their barracks to the Common by the side of Back Bay, even, one story has it, bayoneting a dog that barked; yet surely everybody in town knew what was going on and why. There were anxious faces at many a curtain-slitted window, while anxious ears marked the tramp of feet, muffled though this was.

The boats were waiting, but they were not enough. Two crossings were needed; and at Lechmere's Point, on the other side of the Charles, the men had to wade ashore, knee-deep in water. There, shivering, they waited for something—nobody seemed to know what—for more than an hour, almost two hours.

The winter had been the mildest in human memory, and spring had come early to those parts. All the same, this particular night was a chill one, and the men, not for the first time, cursed the day that they had enlisted—or been pressed.

At last the extra supplies arrived. They were food rations, which the men did not need anyway, for they already had rations. The grumbling subsided to a mumble as the redcoats were lined up. They shouldered their muskets and marched off—into history.

# 3

LEXINGTON was a pretty village of nineteen square miles, 10,000 acres, virtually all of it farmland. It was one of the oldest of Massachusetts settlements, fourteen miles from the sea. Its population was about 750, of whom a little over 200 were able-bodied men between the ages of sixteen and sixty, who, according to law—though there could be a few exceptions, such as preachers of the Gospel and halfwits—were required to serve in the militia. About half of *these*, something between 100 and 120, were classed as minutemen, volunteers who were pledged to turn out at a minute's notice, day or night. This was a system that had been found not very satisfactory, and only a few days earlier the Provincial Congress had decided to discontinue it in favor of a full-time army; but the minuteman system, such as it was, was still in effect the night of April 18–19.

In command, elected by the others, with the rank of captain, was John Parker, a large slow-moving man of forty-five, member of an old Lexington family, a veteran of Rogers' Rangers in the French and Indian War, and the father of seven children.

Revere arrived a little after midnight, and his appearance was by no means unexpected. It is not likely that many of the residents of Lexington were asleep, even at that advanced hour, for rumors had been flying freely, and any thrust at the supply station at Concord from the direction of Boston must be made by way of this village. There was still a light in Buckman's tavern on the highway at the point where this split—north to Bedford, straight ahead for Concord. The point formed by this tavern and by the meetinghouse across from it, on the common proper, were the apex of a triangle, the point at which the invaders would enter the village.

Parker promptly caused the drummer to drum, assembling the minutemen, who came shivering, blinking, asking questions. Most of them clutched muskets, though not all had powder, which was at a premium. The muskets were very long, some more than seven feet, and clumsy to handle. They were of all different calibers, from different countries, a few homemade. It is not likely that there were many powder horns, if there were any at all. The horn was still used on the frontier, but in eastern Massachusetts it was little more than a relic. The minutemen, warned, would have made up their cartridges in advance, measuring out powder in waxed-paper wrappers with a carefully cut ball in each, and stowing these cartridges in cartouche boxes hung at their waists. The powder horn was quaint, but it was unreliable. If in the heat of conflict you poured too much powder into the muzzle of your musket the thing might blow up in your face; whereas if you poured too little it would not propel the ball more than a few feet. With a powder horn the pre-cut balls had to be carried in a separate pouch, an inconvenience that made for longer reloading—and your life might hang on how long it took you to reload. Perhaps most important, the powder horn provided no wadding by means of which the charge could be rammed home; and this had to be sought elsewhere. With a cartridge the leftover waxed paper was a perfect wad.

Parker was perplexed. He lined up his men, such of them as had muskets, the others taking places as spectators around the northern edge of the green. It was no time for speech-making such as would have featured a routine drill, together with a sermon. Parker sent four messengers at separate intervals on horseback along the road toward Menotomy. When these did not return he took it to mean that the alarm had been a false one, and after some hesitation he dismissed the company, warning that everybody should assemble again at the beating of the drum. Some of the men went home, which in no case was very far away, and a few might even have got back into bed; while others made for Buckman's tavern.

Meanwhile Revere had gone to the home of the Reverend Jonas Clark, some distance north of the green but still in or at the edge of the village. This preacher's wife's uncle, John Hancock, the richest man in Boston, conceivably in the whole colony—a fortune inherited from *his* uncle, a man who would be spinning in his grave if he knew the use to which it was being put—was a guest, together with his friend the spellbinder Samuel Adams, who, like Hancock, had found Boston an unhealthy place to be and was hiding out in the country preparatory to starting for Philadelphia and the opening of the Continental Congress. It was understood that these two were so deep in the patriots' plot that they could never wriggle or buy their way out, and it was widely believed that if the British ever did sally forth from Boston it would be as much in the hope of capturing them as in the expectation of destroying the supplies at Concord.

An odder pair it would have been hard to find. Hancock erratic, rich, not too bright, fond of finery, given to histrionics, while Sam Adams, the dowdy, was hard-thinking and poor, a genius at ward politics, steady, a pauseless worker.

There was no candlelight when Revere arrived, and William Munroe, the sergeant of a special guard posted at the Clark house by Captain Parker, shushed him angrily, whispering that the guests wished to have no noise.

"Noise!" Revere exploded. "You'll have noise enough soon! The redcoats are coming!"

Hancock, who must have been intensely awake, overheard this exchange and called out to ask if this was Revere. Revere called that it was indeed, and Hancock cried: "Come in, come in, Revere. We are not afraid of *you!*" King John, as

he was sometimes dubbed because of his pretentiousness and
his peacock strut, was not afraid of anything right then,
unless it was that he should not appear as a shining hero
before his aunt, Mrs. Thomas Hancock, and Miss Dorothy
Quincy, Hancock's skittish young fiancée, who were also
guests that night of the hospitable Reverend Clark. He
spouted sparks and flame. A man of no military experience, he
would have gone out on the green to face the redcoats alone,
his sword in his fist, fire in his eye. He seemed to see nothing
silly in this. It took some time to quiet him. Sam Adams placed
a shaking hand (he suffered from palsy) on King John's
shoulder, and convinced him at last that such behavior would
be playing right into the Britishers' arms. "We are for the
cabinet, you and I," he said, "not for the field of battle." At
last the man consented to be spirited away, complete with
aunt, betrothed, and political protégé, to another house, one
farther from the Lexington-Concord road.

Dawes came soon after Revere, having made good time.[6]
Together, once the Hancock crisis was passed, they started
down the road toward Concord. They were not to get far.

Leaving Lexington at the same time was a spirited young
physician named Samuel Prescott, whom the riders learned
was a right good patriot, "a high son of Liberty," his heart in
the cause. Prescott lived in the Concord to which he was
about to return, but he had not visited Lexington in his professional capacity. He was sparking a Lexington girl, Lydia
Mulliken, whose brother, Nathaniel, a clockmaker, was a
prominent minutemen, out on the green with his musket right
then.[7]

Concord was five to six miles west. Dr. Prescott knew
every resident along the way, and he was a great help in
knocking up minutemen. He was engaged in doing just that,
with Dawes helping him, when Revere, riding ahead, spotted
two British officers. He would not run again! He shouted
back to his companions that they could capture these men,

and he rode toward them. The two suddenly became six, four more appearing from out of the shadows, and all three of the patriots were taken.

Dawes thought fast. He wheeled about so violently that his watch was thrown from his waistcoat pocket. He did not pause to pick it up, but galloped back toward Lexington, two troopers at his heels. He left the road and made for the last house he had just alarmed, shouting as he did so: "Come on, boys! I've got two of them!" It was an old trick, but, incredibly, it worked. The redcoats went back to their officers, and Dawes was free.

A couple of bars were let down from a fence, and Prescott and Revere were ushered into a pasture for what threatened to be a rough questioning session. Prescott, who knew every foot of this country, and whose mount was fresh, suddenly cried "*Put on!*" and wheeled to the left, the direction of Concord. He jumped a low stone wall, and escaped.

Revere tried to do the same thing at the same time, making for a nearby wood, which, alas, before he could reach it, like Birnam came alive, still *more* British officers appearing from out of its darkness; and Revere was irretrievably nabbed.

Officers and sergeants alike, they shook their fists under his nose, cursing him, calling him a rebel, threatening to kill him. The senior officer, one Major Mitchel of the 5th, put a stop to this. Mitchel was a smooth operator. He smiled at Paul Revere. They were not there, he assured the rider, for such honest men as he. They were there only to seek for deserters from the British Army.

Revere laughed in his face. He knew perfectly well what they were doing there, and he told them so. But they would not succeed, he assured them. The expedition had been delayed, he said (which was certainly true); the boats had gone aground (this part he made up); and meanwhile he, Paul Revere, had alerted the entire county. He waved toward nearby Lexington. Did they know how many men were in arms and waiting there? Five hundred! Maybe more!

They were impressed. They already knew that Smith was late: it was almost dawn, and they could hear no tramping feet. If there were anywhere near as many armed men waiting on Lexington common as this fellow said, then there would surely be at least a brush, conceivably a full-scale slaughter. Major Mitchel decided that they had better circle the village and get on the Menotomy road, to warn the oncoming soldiery.

A sergeant with a pistol had been assigned to watch Revere and to blow his head off if he tried again to run, but now this man was relieved. Revere was told to dismount, and he was left standing in the middle of the field, a sorry ending to his ride.

The deacon in Charlestown never did see his horse again, nor William Dawes his watch.

# 4

G AGE WAS A CAREFUL PLANNER, and as soon as he had made up the original invasion party, the light infantry and the grenadiers, he proceeded to make up a supplementary force by means of which they could be relieved or reinforced if reinforcement or relief was called for. A large portion of this second party was to be marines.

Colonel Smith, what with the delay at Lechmere's Point, and what with the fact that the countryside all around them appeared to have been raised against them, as was evidenced by the lighted windows and the ringing of church bells, decided early that he could use that secondary force; and he sent back for it. Then he slogged on toward Menotomy.

Menotomy was all lit up, and they were watched from every window as they passed. It was in Menotomy that the Committee of Safety of the Provincial Congress had been meeting as recently as the previous day, and three members of that body still were there, lodged at the inn. These three failed at first to realize that their presence might be known or at least suspected by the redcoats, who indeed might have been sent out of Boston for the very purpose of rounding up a few arch-rebels like them. Not until they saw an officer and a squad of men peel off from the column and approach the inn did they take alarm. Then there was something like a panic. One of the delegates, the erratic Elbridge Gerry,[8] in his excitement started for the front door, which would have precipitated him right into the arms of the redcoats. "For God's sake, don't open that door!" the landlord shouted; and he guided them to a back door that opened upon a field of cut corn. There was no cover nearby, and the three threw themselves flat upon the earth among the stubble. It was an uncomfortable quarter-hour, in their nightshirts, but it was better than being hanged.

On the far side of Menotomy, Colonel Smith halted his men to give them a brief rest and also to harangue them on the need for speed. The troops, in truth, had done very well: it was the delay at Lechmere's Point that had put them behind in their schedule.

It would be dawn by the time they reached the next town, Lexington, the last before Concord, and Colonel Smith feared, the countryside being in a state of alarm, that they might meet opposition there. He sent Major Pitcairn and six companies of light infantry ahead with orders to seize everyone they encountered. These men did not march in conventional fashion, down the middle of the road, as they had been doing, but spread out on both sides, so that they were not readily seen. It was in this way that they snapped up the first three of Captain Parker's scouts, while Parker waited in vain for a report.

The fourth scout, however, eluded them. This was a lad named Thaddeus Bowman, and though he did not at first see the men who lurked in the shadows of the trees alongside the road, his horse did see them, or smelled them, or in some manner sensed them; and the horse refused to go on. Then Bowman saw in the moonlight far ahead the solid column of the grenadiers, who *did* march down the middle of the road, and he turned and galloped back to Lexington, shouting the news.

They must have been very near the village, for in a matter of minutes they heard the rattle of a drum and a few odd shots. The shots were intended to summon back to the common such militiamen as might be sleeping nearby, but for all Pitcairn knew they might have been fired in defiance.

To make matters worse, at just this time one of the men

reported seeing a flash-in-the-pan in the shadows that lined the road just ahead. Was that meant to be a signal, a warning? or had somebody deliberately tried to fire upon His Majesty's soldiers?

Then Major Mitchel and his fellow officers appeared, having hooked around the village, and they passed on Paul Revere's cock-and-bull story about 500 or more armed militiamen lined up on the green just ahead.

It was too much for Major Pitcairn, who ordered his troopers to stop and to load.

This was a complex process. The standard British infantry weapon was the Brown Bess musket, so called because not only the walnut stock but the barrel as well were brown, the metal having been treated with a preservative. It was 3 feet 8 inches long in the barrel, more than 5 feet overall, a marvel of compactness, without the bayonet, and could not be loaded in a kneeling or sitting position, much less prone, for it had to be held upright, the muzzle high, the butt on the ground. Each soldier took a paper cartridge, of which he carried sixty, and tore it open with his teeth. He pured the powder into the gun muzzle and dropped the ball on top of it, afterward crumpling the paper and ramrodding this in as a wad. Then he lifted the frizzen, or lid, from his firing pan, and by batting the barrel with the heel of his hand caused a little powder to puff through the touchhole and into the pan. Now he was ready to fire.

A really good soldier—but he had to be *very* good—could fire and reload in fifteen seconds. He did not aim at anything: the Brown Bess did not even have back sights. He was trained only to point the weapon in the general direction of the enemy, turn his head away if there was any kind of wind for fear of a flareback through the touchhole that might take away his eyebrows or even his eyes, and pull the trigger, or "tricker," at an officer's command. Everything was controlled firepower, volley shooting.

After they had loaded their muskets, Major Pitcairn's men fixed their bayonets. The bayonet was 13 inches long and weighed 1 pound 2 ounces: the musket itself, without the bayonet, weighed 14 pounds.

Then they were carefully and loudly ordered (and John Parker was giving his men exactly the same order at the same time, up the road a piece): "Don't shoot unless you are shot at."

They shouldered arms and resumed the march in proper parade fashion. Marching in ranks with loaded guns and fixed bayonets was a risky business, the locks being what they were; but this was an emergency.

A large white church-meetinghouse blocked the eastern point of the triangle that was the green at Lexington. They passed around this on both sides, and when in the dawn's early light they saw the double file of minutemen a hundred yards ahead they brought their arms to port position and broke into a trot, screaming obscenities.

# 5

Profanity suits the soldier. Whether it quiets his latent fear or whether he believes that it proves his he-manliness to any who might be interested, the serviceman, officer or ranker, has always splattered verbal smut about him like a child splattering mud.

The people of Boston, who like most New Englanders esteemed the third to be one of the most important of the commandments brought down from Sinai, had never ceased to wince at these foulmouthed fighters who did not mutter but *shouted* their oaths. To the people of quiet little God-fearing Lexington it was something new, and to be charged by an army with billingsgate must have been as appalling as to be charged by an army with banners and long lances.

Captain Parker's strung-out double line held, but it wavered under the impact of such filth. Many of the men, whether from fear or poor hearing, had not returned when the drum was beaten for the second alarm. Others were spectators, having no guns. At least three were in the meeting-house looking for powder when the scarlet wave burst upon them.

There were not one hundred men in Parker's line. There might have been barely seventy.

The redcoats ground to a halt a few feet from the narrow line, and they stood there shaking their fists, waving their muskets, and screeching abuse at the bewildered, shocked Yankees. Their officers did nothing to stop them.

Despite the noise, Major Pitcairn was heard when he

bellowed from his horse: *"Lay down your arms, you damn' rebels! Lay down your arms and disperse!"*

It was the least that he could do. He could hardly ask his men to turn their backs on an arrangement like this.

Captain Parker ordered his men to disperse. They started to obey him, with a few exceptions, drifting apart in a highly unmilitary manner. But nobody put down his musket. Muskets cost money.

Then, at this touchy moment, somebody fired a shot. Whether it was a Britisher or an American who did so, whether a spectator, a militiaman, or a redcoat, we shall never know. It might have been meant for a signal of some sort, or for a threat, or it might have been an accident. It does not matter. The thing was bound to happen, tempers being what they were.

Instantly the front-line redcoats leveled their guns and fired point-blank at Parker's men, most of whom were leaving the common.

Old Jabez Parker, a cousin of the captain, had placed a tricornful of cartridges between his feet and had vowed that he would not retreat from any lobsterback. Nor did he. He was shot where he stood. From a prone position, still alive, he fired, hitting nothing. He was bayoneted to death—from behind.

Jonathan Harrington made it to his own house, only a few hundred feet away, on hands and knees, trailing blood. In the open doorway his wife and eight-year-old son, horrified, watched him crawl toward them. He collapsed at their feet, dead.

In all, eight were killed, most of them being shot in the back. Nine were wounded. British casualties consisted of two superficial skin grooves, one in a private's leg, the other in the belly of Major Pitcairn's horse.

Very few of the Americans fired, but the redcoats had gone mad, hysterical, and seemed to think that they were

THE BATTLE OF LEXINGTON

being shot at from the nearby houses, which they proposed to break into. In fact, there were only women and children in those houses. Nor had anybody holed up at Buckman's. Of the three men trapped in the meetinghouse, two broke out and sprinted for safety, bullets whizzing past their ears. One made it; the other was killed. The third, Joshua Simonds, inside the meetinghouse, thrust the muzzle of his musket into an open barrel of gunpowder and watched the doorway, determined to blow up the whole place the moment the British came in. The British never did go in there. Neither did they go to the Reverend Jonas Clark's house on the Bedford road several hundred yards northwest of the common, the house Sam Adams and John Hancock had so hurriedly vacated.

It was touch-and-go for a little while there, with the redcoats, heedless of their officers, acting like a mob, threatening to break into every house in the village. It was only when Colonel Smith came up with the grenadiers—the light infantry from his own 10th Regiment had been among the worst of the offenders—that he and Pitcairn and some of the younger officers managed to get the men back into line. At the edge of the common, with the air still choky with gunsmoke, the officers dressed them down, though they did not go so far as to tell the men—what would have been the truth—that they had disgraced their uniform; but afterward they did permit them to fire a triumphant volley into the air, and to give, in accordance with the British Army tradition, three rousing cheers for the glorious victory they had just won. Then they started down the road for Concord.

That was Lexington. It was not a battle, not even a skirmish. It was, simply, a massacre.

One by one, grim and silent, the minutemen came out of the places where they had hid. They carried the dead back to their homes, and treated the wounded. They cleared the common. They took, separately, five prisoners, redcoats who had lingered either to loot or, more likely, had seized this chance to desert.[9] The British would be back in Lexington before the day was out—they'd have to, going from Concord to Boston—and so the women and children who lived in the village were escorted to far-out farmhouses for the present, and coins and silver plate were buried.

The boy William Diamond was ordered to beat his drum again, and in this way the militiamen were summoned, what was left of them, some in bandages, for the third time. They were lined up by Captain Parker and Sergeant Munroe, their arms and ammunition checked, and with the drum drumming and all of them studiously striving to keep in step, they started down the road toward Concord.

The fight wasn't over yet.

# 6

It was a bright clear morning, coolish, gusty. The sky was a helter-skelter of small puffy white clouds. The sun, expanding, promised warmth a little later.

Concord was a town about twice the size of Lexington, between five and six miles away. It was not flat like Lexington. A high ridge ran along the northern side of the village, and along the western edge ran the Concord River, scarcely more than an oversized brook, which was crossed by two bridges—the North Bridge and the South Bridge, the latter being nearer the center of the village. Lieutenant Colonel Smith knew all this, for he had seen the maps made by the two young officers "disguised as countrymen." What Smith did *not* know was that as a result of a special trip to Concord the previous Sunday, when Revere warned the town of the British preparations, a large part of the supplies had been hidden or moved away.

Smith's men had been on their feet for ten hours now, but still they marched well. After the excruciating boredom of Boston, it was good to swing their legs.

The immediate alarm, the news that the redcoats were actually on their way, had been given by the fast-riding Dr. Prescott at about one o'clock in the morning, after he had escaped from Revere's captors. Prescott, on his way, had knocked up the village of Lincoln, where there was a militia company that soon joined the two companies in Concord. There were about 250 men, all armed. Others would surely come, for the word was being spread.

There was no snapping of orders, no scurrying of aides. It was more like an open-air town meeting, with everybody speaking his mind, privates and officers together. They were very serious about it, and subdued. There might have been a few Tories in Concord, but if so they kept their mouths shut, for the town, if not unanimous like Lexington, was predominantly patriotic.

The Reverend William Emerson[10] because of his cloth was not required to carry a musket in the militia, but he did carry one all the same, and had been among the very first on the scene. He was all for marching forth to meet the British, and there were others who felt the same way, though many thought that if there was to be a war it would be better to let the other side start it.

A little before dawn they sent Reuben Brown, a harness maker, in the direction of Lexington, to learn whether there had been any resistance. Reuben returned to report that he had heard firing on the green but had not ventured near enough to determine whether the British were using ball and not just wadding. (There were many among the minutemen who could not bring themselves to believe that the redcoats would use "live" ammunition against what were, after all, fellow Englishmen.)

The hawks and the doves had at it again, and the hawks triumphed, temporarily. It was decided that they should march out and meet the British. No further plans than this were made.

Each company had its drummer, and each drummer was busy. After a while they saw the British, not much more than half a mile ahead, stepping along briskly, glittering in the early sun. The Yankees halted, not in fear but thoughtfully; and once again they had a conference. The force coming toward them was almost three times the size of their own, though reinforcements could be expected at any hour from the towns west of Concord. If they were to dispute passage of the road, it would be the same as firing the first shot, wouldn't it?

There was no hint of panic. They talked it over, there in the roadway, briefly but quietly; and they decided to turn around and march back into town. They did not hurry. They kept step very well, for amateurs; and the drums were drumming all the while.

Just a few hundred yards behind them the British kept coming on . . . and on . . . a bright clockwork.

The British met no opposition then, but the ridge on their right was peppered with peering patriots, each carrying his long musket; and this, understandably, made Colonel Smith nervous. The colonel dispatched some of the light infantrymen up to that rise to clear it. They had no trouble doing so. The minutemen did not shoot or even make menacing gestures; but simply melted away, to reassemble a little later on Punkatasset Hill just the other side of the North Bridge. This was a good place for them. They could look down into the town. They could greet oncoming companies from other towns. They could keep an eye on the bridge, and they could threaten the road to the home of Colonel James Barrett, west of the river, where a large part of the supplies had been stored.

There were about 400 of the militiamen now. They consisted of six companies, two from Concord and one each from Carlisle, Lincoln, Bedford, and Acton. They didn't do anything, just stood there and watched.

In the town Colonel Smith divided his forces. Of the ten companies of light infantry at his command, each company consisting nominally of 28 men, he sent one to guard the South Bridge, kept two on hand as a reserve, and dispatched the other seven to guard the North Bridge and search Colonel Barrett's house on the other side of the river.

If there was going to be trouble, the North Bridge was the logical place for it. It was behind this bridge that the disquietingly silent rebels were massed. It would be necessary to cross the bridge in order to get to the home of Colonel Barrett, who was not only the custodian of so much of the military supplies but also commanding officer of the militia in this vicinity.

There was not the slightest sign of resistance within the village itself, where there remained only women and children and very old men.

Yet Colonel Smith not only did not accompany the party to the North Bridge; he did not even send with it his second-in-command, that experienced warrior Major Pitcairn. The seven companies of light infantry were under their respective captains, with Parsons of the 10th in overall command.

Parsons stationed only one company at the bridge itself, on the far side of it, the side toward Punkatasset Hill, where the rebels stood in silence, leaning on their long guns, unpredictable. Two other companies he stationed in some low hills down the road toward the Barrett farm, which was about two miles away. All three of these companies were put under the command of Captain Walter Laurie of the 43rd.

Parsons himself led the remaining companies to the home of Colonel Barrett, which was deserted. All they found was a couple of 24-pounders, too heavy to be hauled away in a hurry. They knocked the trunnions off these, disabling them as best they could, though not putting them out of operation altogether. For the rest, search as they would they could find nothing that by any stretch of imagination could be classed as military supplies. It was discouraging, after that long walk.

Meanwhile Captain Laurie was getting uneasy, for he could see that the men who hung on the side of the hill were huddling in conferences that boded no good for his thin force. He called in the other two companies, stationed down the road, and ordered all three companies across the bridge to the east side, the side toward the village. Even then he was uneasy, for he saw the men on the hill assembling in some sort of order, plainly preparing to march. He sent to Colonel Smith in the village, asking for reinforcements.

Smith responded by ordering out a company of grenadiers, which he led in person; but characteristically he was late.

In the village all went well. Their officers had hammered

into the grenadiers that there simply must not be another
disgusting scene such as the one in Lexington. At all costs the
feelings of the civilians must be considered. Anything that
was taken, except in the way of military supplies, must be
paid for. This was a hard order to obey, for the troops were
hungry, and the town afforded fresh milk and eggs, freshly
baked bread and cakes, great delicacies for men who had been
subsisting on salt pork and sour beer. But they obeyed,
officers and men, and they paid what was asked. The townspeople sniffed at the proffered coins as "blood money" and
"contaminated silver"; but they took them.

Very little else was found. The searchers missed the
provincial money chest, which had been left at the local inn a
few days before by the treasurer, Henry Gardner: a young
woman insisted that it was hers and that it was private
property, and they believed her, not investigating. At the
Woods house near the South Bridge the womenfolk told
them that there was one room they hoped would not be
searched, for it was occupied by a sick woman, so the grenadiers tiptoed past that portal, thus missing the only military
supplies in the place.

So it went. They got pitifully little for their pains.

Of course they chopped down the Liberty Pole, this
being an act that always gave them great satisfaction, though
they must have known that another would be erected as soon
as they had gone away.

In the yard of the jail they did find three 24-pounders,
which they spiked, afterward burning the wooden carriages.
They confiscated about 100 barrels of flour, and they started
to stave these in, one by one, and to scatter their contents in
the dust. But this was a lot of work; and they ended by
rolling most of the barrels into the village millpond, where the
water made a paste of the outer flour, sealing the cracks in the
barrels, which were thereby made waterproof, so that the
villagers later were able to retrieve nine-tenths of the stuff.

"And the men may put balls or lead in their pockets,

throwing them by degrees into ponds, ditches, etc., but in no quantity together so that they may be recovered afterwards," Gage had written in his orders to Colonel Smith. But the men had heavy knapsacks, and they had their muskets,[11] and when they seized about 500 pounds in musket balls they simply tossed these into the millpond after the flour. The townsmen raked them out as soon as the red backs were turned.

About the only other supplies seized were some entrenching tools, of which the soldiers burned the wooden handles in the same fire that they had used for the gun carriages.

It was this fire that brought about the battle.

The men on Punkatasset Hill could see the smoke but not the fire itself, and they not unnaturally jumped to the conclusion that the redcoats had started to burn the town. That was too much. What kind of men were they if they would stand apart and aloof while their wives and children, not to mention their homes, were incinerated? They formed into companies and marched down the hill.

They were orderly about it, if not smart. They kept in step. They might have numbered 500 by this time, for they had been joined by individual militiamen from nearby villages —Littleton, Chelmsford, Westford. At the rear, sitting his horse, was Colonel Barrett, who had given them last-minute orders not to fire unless fired upon. At the head of the column was a small boy from Acton, who gaily piped on a fife.

Some of the redcoats started to pull up the planks of the bridge, apparently forgetting all about the men at Colonel Barrett's house, but a Concord officer, Major Buttrick, called out to them to stop. They stopped, not because of his order but because they were startled to see how near at hand the rebels were, and they were scared.

The Americans stopped on the far side of the river. There was a distance of about fifty yards between the front-rank men.

What Captain Laurie was thinking when he placed his

THE FIGHT AT CONCORD BRIDGE

men—if indeed he was thinking at all—we shall never know. They were jammed together so tight that most of them could not even bring their muskets to bear. It may be that Laurie had called for "street firing," a recently developed tactic by means of which a column of four or more in close formation advanced up a narrow space—or retreated along such a space. The front rank fires, and then splits and goes around to the rear, there to reload while the next rank fires, splits, and goes around to the rear. "Street firing" called for a great deal of training, which presumably these men, including Laurie, did not have. This was not the place for such a tactic anyway.

There was no question, this time, about who fired first. The British did. They fired four or five scattered shots into the river, perhaps meaning them as a threat. Then they fired a straight-ahead volley.

Captain Isaac Davis and another Acton man, Abner Hosmer, a private, fell dead. The fifer boy was knocked down, badly wounded.

"God damn it, they're firing ball!" cried a Concord captain, Timothy Brown, as he heard the lead whistling past his ears: he was one of those who until the last minute had refused to believe that the British really meant it.

Major Buttrick shouted an order to fire, and there was a volley from the American side of the stream.

Then a strange thing happened. True, the British were outnumbered five to one, though they could assume that reinforcements were on the way. True, they had been poorly handled, poorly led. But they had their bayonets, and most of them still had loaded muskets, for only a few in the front ranks had fired. The Americans could only have crossed the bridge three or four abreast, and the surrounding fields afforded many trees and stone walls behind which to fight.

Anyway, the British turned and ran, every man jack of them. They bolted like rabbits from the shot that was heard round the world.

# 7

THE MINUTEMEN did not follow up the rout, even though it clearly was complete, the redcoats not even pausing to help their wounded, who hobbled along as best they could, or to take care of the two men who were dead and the one who was dying, groaning, near the bridge. The minutemen crossed that bridge, and stepped gingerly around the bodies, which they did not touch.

Their late adversaries had met Colonel Smith and his grenadiers at the edge of the village, but the commander made no attempt to rally them, only conducted them back into town, doing nothing about the dead and wounded, and apparently forgetting the men Parsons had taken to the Barrett farm.

The minutemen could see this. They could see into the village now, too, and they perceived that the fires, of which they had previously spotted only the smoke, were no more than bonfires. This satisfied them, for the present. They broke into little groups, no longer pretending to exercise martial order. Some of them drifted along the top of the northern ridge, from where they could watch the village and be ready for anything that might happen. Others went back over the bridge and picked up and carried away their own dead and wounded, after which they scattered across the countryside, scrounging for food, for it was by now the middle of the morning, and these men had been up since before dawn without any chance to get breakfast.

The whole fight had taken only a few minutes, and now

the vicinity of the bridge was deserted except for the two dead men and the poor wretch groaning his life away.

A harum-scarum country lad came timorously across the bridge from the west, and he had a hatchet in his hand. He had been splitting firewood nearby, and he came to see what all the shooting was about. He had scarcely got across the bridge when the dying man groaned again. The lad jumped, scared. Then, whether in a paroxysm of rage or because he thought he was defending himself, the boy stove in the dying man's skull, after which he ran away.

When Captain Parsons and his men returned from the Barrett farm—not knowing that there was anything wrong, they had stopped at a country tavern for a drink before starting the return march—they were astounded to see that some of the planks were missing from the bridge, and equally astounded by the sight of the three bodies. They hastened on to the village. It was left for the rebels to bury the British dead.

Wild stories have always swirled like smoke through armies, the members of which for long stretches of time have little else to do but listen to them and pass them on. Most are immediately lost, and good riddance. They might have been mildly useful for recreational purposes when there was no real action, but they were soon forgotten.

It was not so with the story that Parsons' men brought away from the North Bridge. They solemnly averred, every one of them, that they had seen a wounded man who had been scalped, the way the red Indians scalp their victims. Soon they added—or others who passed the tale along added—that not only had the poor devil's hair been removed, together with the skin that held it, but his ears had been cut off too. One variant had it that the eyes of the still living man had been gouged out as well. Nobody pooh-poohed this. Nobody went back to the bridge to verify it—or conceivably to do something for the man who was dying—but it was almost unanimously believed, by officers and men alike.

It made a big change, this story, in the attitude of the British toward their foes. They had come to Concord sneeringly, esteeming the "countrymen" to be the stupidest sort of bumpkins, oafs, louts, doodles,[12] but essentially, howsoever comic, harmless. Now they looked upon them as savages. The new attitude, which was to spread throughout the whole British Army in America, made a great deal of difference in the war.

There was plenty of time for it to circulate immediately after its miraculous birth, as Colonel Smith did not seem to know what to do with his men, and he wasted a good two hours in Concord. His outposts were in. He had destroyed all the military supplies he could lay hands on. He certainly was not going to venture out into the countryside in an attempt to disperse the seemingly aimless groups of musket-trailing men who were everywhere around Concord now. Time after time he paraded the redcoats on the green, but that was simply in order to look busy. What he really was doing was wasting time in the hope that his relief would arrive before he had to start that horrid trip back to Boston. The relief should have been there two hours ago. Something, he sighed to himself, must have gone wrong.

Time was working against Smith, but it was working for the rebels, despite the fact that they too did virtually nothing throughout those two hours—for instance, they did not annoy Parsons' men when these came back from Barrett's, though they outnumbered them by five or six to one and could easily have controlled the bridge. The minutemen no doubt were waiting for the redcoats to get out of Concord, fearful that if attacked there they would fire the town, their hostage. There was no master plan; there were no maneuvers. No one man was in command. Colonel Barrett, nominally the head of the militia in those parts, had accepted this post only with the understanding that he would be called upon for nothing but advice and would not be expected to take the field physically: he was sixty-five. Major Buttrick kept his own Concord men more or less around him, but they tried nothing, only watched. The others wandered where they would, taking orders from nobody. There was no head-quarters, no supply depot.

Still, this amorphous force at least was growing larger all the time. They were coming in from all around—from Sud-bury, Woburn, Billerica, Framingham, Reading. They were in small groups, but they moved fast, cutting across fields, some of them even dogtrotting part of the way, fully earning their penny-a-mile road allowance.

Some of these swarms, differently equipped, could have been used to better advantage elsewhere. The average militia-man was as handy with an ax as he was with a spade, and he knew both of these instruments better than he knew the musket that ordinarily he handled only in a drill or fired in the exuberance of a drill-day salute. This raid upon the stores at Concord had been expected for some time, and a few officers, if there had been any sensible central command, could easily have surveyed the roads between Concord on the west and Cambridge, Lechmere's Point, and Charlestown on the east, and selected the best place for tree fellings. A handful of ax experts, when the big day did come, could have done more to entangle and distress the British than could a whole army of undisciplined musketeers. Such fellings too, at the narrow places, would greatly impede the advance of a relief column. It was not done because nobody thought of it.

At last Smith did start out, no fifes or drums, no flags. The redcoats were not even talking to one another. As before, the grenadiers stayed on the road while the light infantry scrambled along the spur of high land, on the left now, on the north. This spur of land extended for about a mile out of the village to a fork called Meriam's Corner, and it was there that all hell broke loose.

CHAPTER

8

AN INSIGNIFICANT STREAM cut the road at this point, and there was a narrow wooden bridge over it. When members of the British rear guard had passed across this bridge, they turned, raising their muskets. They might have meant this merely as a threatening gesture. They might have intended to fire a volley into the air as a warning. Or perhaps they really were looking for trouble; and if they were, they got it.

There was a splatter of explosions, and men fell on both sides.

The Yankee wounded were in home country and would be cared for, but the British were obliged to carry their wounded with them lest they be scalped and otherwise mutilated. These were sent forward, the van being the safest place in a retreat, to join the other wounded, some of whom were in chaises. That unsteady group of those who had been hit, with a single file of soldiers on either side, was to increase mightily as the day wore on. The dead were simply left behind.

The brush at the North Bridge and the exchange of shots at Meriam's Corner were the only stand-up fights of that long, bitter day. After Meriam's Corner the Americans split into two groups—those who went on the right, and those who went on the left—and they stayed a short distance from the British flanks, crouching behind walls, trees, outbuildings. A man would fire, duck, reload, and then, bent low, protected by a wall or a wood, run to another firing place forward; and

MINUTEMEN FIGHTING FROM BEHIND WALLS AND TREES

he would keep this up as long as his ammunition lasted, after which he would go home, for no powder or ball was distributed on the field, no supplies of any sort. New minutemen were pouring in all the time, but old ones were going away. A few of the captains made some effort to control their companies, to keep order, but for the most part it was every man for himself.

This was Indian fighting, the kind that came naturally to Americans. To the British, trained to European standards, it was not war at all, simply murder. Anybody, any wild-eyed peasant, who—they believed—would scalp his prisoners alive and then kneel behind a wall[13] to shoot at the King's soldiers, was not a man at all. He was merely a beast, and should be treated as such. The British were furious.

Flanking parties were thrown out to try to get around the Yankees, and in some cases they did. A light infantry sergeant, coming suddenly upon Jonathan Wilson of Bedford, who was reloading behind a barn, unhesitatingly shot him dead—in the back. Why not? They had both been standing upright, hadn't they?

Most of the countrymen's shots were wasted, not because the countrymen fired too high—a common fault with untrained soldiers—but because they fired from too far away. A reasonably good musket might carry for a hundred yards or even a little longer, but its *effective* range was only about sixty to seventy yards. After that the ball was "spent," no more harmful than a tossed pebble. On the other hand, except for a few of the light infantry's outflanking parties' shots, virtually *all* the fire from the British side was wasted. The redcoats were bewildered. They had been trained to fire in volleys at command, and who had ever known a fight like this? They would see a head, an arm, the muzzle of a musket, then a smear of greasy gray smoke. Before they could swing their own muskets into position, everything but the smoke had gone, and there was nothing to shoot *at*. They seemed to think that their blind blazing away might frighten the Yankees, but it did not have that effect.

The officers tried to stop this wild firing, which was using up ammunition at a frightful rate, but the officers were not very effective. For one thing, many of them had been put out of action. Colonel Smith himself was shot in the leg, and when he tried to ride his horse he drew such a hot fire from behind those stone walls that he had to get down again and hobble along like anybody else, which was hard on a man of his flesh. Major Pitcairn's horse, grazed in the tussle on Lexington green, bolted at an extra-loud, too-near burst of musketry, and threw him. The major was unhurt, but the horse escaped to the rebel lines.[14] Epaulets were easily spotted, and casualties among the officers were especially high. Four of the eight officers who had been at the North Bridge, for instance, were in the wounded column before the departure from Concord.

About the time that they passed the hamlet of Lincoln, halfway between Concord and Lexington, they noted an increase in the musketry on the right. Had they but known it, these were the very men upon whom they had fired earlier that day, at dawn. John Parker's company had come to join the battle.[15]

There was one irregular group of Americans that did not indulge in Indian fighting. These marched right down the middle of the road behind the British—but comfortably behind, out of musket range, a sort of mopping-up squad that pounced upon stragglers and caused the British rear guard to waste an unconscionable amount of ammunition.

On both sides of the road, though you seldom saw anybody, the musketry increased. The whole countryside must be swarming in on this column like angry bees. They gave an impression, these invisible ones, of a horde, albeit a widely dispersed horde. (Ensign De Bernière, no fool, was to calculate their numbers as at least 5,000: in point of fact, there was never, at any one time, a quarter of that number.)

That the ammunition was almost gone must have come as a terrible blow. It had never happened before to the British Army, each soldier of which, following the example of the master, Frederick of Prussia, carried sixty cartridges when he set forth; and who ever heard of firing more than sixty shots of an afternoon?

They started to run. It was little more than a nervous trot at first; but it quickened, weary though the men were. The officers flourished their swords, beat legs, to no avail. It would soon be a stampede.

They would be lucky if they got back to Lexington, much less Boston, and they all knew it. They had been on their feet for fourteen hours and had covered about thirty miles, lugging all the while their rifles, knapsacks, and cartouche boxes, to the weight of about 125 pounds a man. They could hardly stand; yet they tried to run.

Would they surrender right on Lexington green? That would be poetic justice perhaps, but it would be damned unpleasant.

Stumbling, they entered the village.

There was the hoarse cough of a 6-pounder the other side of the meetinghouse, on the road to Menotomy. The ball thudded somewhere just behind where the rebels must be, and the musketry ceased.

There was another cough . . . and another. . . .

The relief had arrived.

# 9

As Smith gloomily predicted, something had gone wrong.

Before he went to bed the night of the 18th, General Gage had given orders that the relief force, whether needed or not, was to be paraded on the common at four o'clock in the morning. It was to consist of three regiments of infantry (minus, of course, their flank companies, which were in the field), one battalion of marines, and a detachment of the Royal Artillery with two 6-pounders. This would make a force about the size of the one already at work or slightly larger—700 to 800 men. The commanding officer was to be Gage's adjutant general, Colonel Hugh Percy, son and heir of the Duke of Northumberland, and an earl in his own right. Lord Percy was no effete aristocrat, and not an absentee owner of his colonelcy. In his lower thirties, he was a vigorous, full-time professional soldier, a man who got things done. The botchery of April 19 in the morning must have caused him real pain.

In the first place, the original order had been misplaced or else lost. At four o'clock in the morning there was nobody on Boston Common. This became the more serious when, at a little after five, Colonel Smith's request for reinforcements arrived and the matter became an emergency, not just a routine turning-out.

It was almost seven o'clock before the artillery and the infantry regiments at last assembled on the common, and even then the marines were missing. Knocked up, the marines denied that they were late: they had never been summoned, they said. It turned out that the summons had been directed to their commanding officer *personally* rather than as commanding officer. This was no other than Major Pitcairn, who was already in the field, a fact that nobody seemed to have noticed.

There was not even a show of secrecy about this expedition—there could hardly be—and when it marched out over Boston Neck, at nine o'clock, there were hundreds to watch and to cheer or jeer it.

The bridge over the Charles River at Cambridge had been dismantled, but the stringpieces were still in place and the planks had been neatly piled on the far bank, so that not much time was spent making temporary repairs. Percy left behind his supply wagon with men to complete this repair job, for he expected to be back soon. (This proved to be a mistake, for the wagon was seized, with the supplies, and one of the guards was killed and the others taken prisoner, when the wagon, trying to catch up to the main column, was set upon at Menotomy by a group of old men, all who were left.)

Had Percy's departure been made on time, or if it had been made only half as late as in fact it was made, he might not have had to pause at the Cambridge bridge, he might not have lost his supply wagon, and certainly he would have joined Smith at Concord rather than at Lexington. On the other hand, if he had been only a *little* later Smith's whole command would have had to surrender and Percy's column would have been lucky to get back.

A great host of countrymen had come in during those two hours when a frustrated Smith waited in vain at Concord.

Untrained troops were notoriously fearful of cannon fire, and Percy made full use of his 6-pounders as he approached Lexington. In the village itself, the patriots for the time being halted, he formed his soldiers into a hollow square and gave the poor men from Concord a chance to drop panting to the ground. He set fire to two houses there (one of them Lydia Mulliken's) not out of savagery—he was not a savage man—but in order to cover his retreat. Once he had started those 6-pounders on the road back, he would be subject to the same harassment that Smith had suffered all the way from Concord, and he knew this. Peasants were appearing from everywhere; it sometimes looked as though they must have dropped out of the sky. More than forty villages and towns sent men into that fight, but they constantly came and went, and it is not likely that there were ever more than about 1,350 Americans taking part in the battle at one time—about the number of the British. They only *seemed* innumerable.

Percy allowed half an hour for the rest, and then they started back toward Menotomy.

It was hell, that march. The wounded, the limpers, those who had to be carried, increased in numbers all the time. The whole column staggered. The countryside perfectly favored its defenders, what with hills, narrow lanes, stone walls, and in Menotomy the houses. The British were especially furious about being fired at from houses, and the orders were to kill anybody found in any structure from which a shot had come.

The fighting was fiercest in Menotomy, where several hundred fresh countrymen appeared. There was a great deal of door-to-door combat. The British, undoubtedly under orders, would enter any house from which they had been fired upon, or thought that they had been fired upon, and they would bayonet anybody they found there. Usually they found nobody. There was very little looting: there simply was not time for looting. The same thing applied to setting fire to the house from which an attack had been made. Such fires were authorized "had there been time to kindle any,"[16] but all the redcoats knew that if they did not regain the protection of their guns in Boston by nightfall they were doomed.

Just beyond Menotomy, to the east, the road branched, going right to Cambridge, left to Charlestown. Percy had come by way of Cambridge, but he decided to go back by way of Charlestown. It was shorter, for one thing, and minutes counted now. Also, he feared that the bridge at Cambridge might have been dismantled again, or that it might be defended.

In truth, the only general officer on the American side, William Heath of Roxbury, a short, fat, bald-headed man, a little earlier had managed to divert some of the north-coming companies of minutemen to the Cambridge bridge, where they might well have given Percy a bad time. It was almost the only *thought-ahead* on the part of any of the Americans. Everything else was spontaneous.

Heath, a farmer of little originality but with vast enthusiasm for the military art, had his own ideas about what should have been done that momentous afternoon, but though he held the rank of major general in the Massachusetts militia, he had no aides, he had no staff, and how could he see that his orders were carried out?

At that fork in the road there stood a tavern run by a man named Benjamin Cooper. Two of the town's leading topers, the brothers-in-law Jason Winship and Jabez Wyman, were comfortably drinking there; and when the battle approached, the keeper and his wife urged them to go down the cellar, as the Coopers themselves were about to do. They shook their heads. No, the British wouldn't bother them.

Outside, a neighboring farmer, Samuel Whittemore, used the end of the tavern as a cover for taking a pop at the redcoats as they passed. Whittemore had a musket but he was not a member of the militia, which did not take men over sixty. Whittemore was seventy-eight years old, the father of nine children, one of whom, a daughter, had presented him with *thirty-six* grandchildren. Now he fired. He had started to reload, when a group of redcoats came on the run. They knocked him down, and beat him with their gun butts, and ran him through repeatedly with their bayonets, leaving him at last for dead. The redcoats then plunged into the tavern, where the fuzzy-eyed brothers-in-law were killed, very messily, where they sat. (*They* were indubitably dead when the redcoats went away, but Sam Whittemore lived to be ninety-six, and to his dying day he swore that he would have done the same thing over again if the circumstances suggested it.)

At long last, just as the sun was setting, the British reached and crossed Charlestown Neck, where they came under the protection of the warships in the bay. They dropped, exhausted.

The score: British 73 killed, 174 wounded; Americans 49 killed, 39 wounded. But there was a lot more to it than that.

# 10

A SIEGE is supposed to be a thought-out thing, a well-planned thing, the result of elaborate preparation. To speak of a "spontaneous siege" is to use a contradiction of terms. Yet this was a "spontaneous siege."

A siege calls for an enormous train of heavy cannon, and the Continentals had only a few small old iron pieces, a few moldering mortars. A siege assumed lines of circumvallation, a huge stock of gabions and fascines, and entrenching tools for the building of breastworks in accordance with a preplotted layout. It calls for magazines and storage space, for supply lines of all sorts. The rebels had none of these.

A siege assumed that a place—a town, a city, a fort, or whatnot—is to be *taken*. There was no thought of taking Boston. The place was heavily fortified, and it was almost completely surrounded by water, over which the defenders had full control. Thus, it was a containment rather than a siege. No order had been given, no campaign mapped. The minutemen had acted without direction or any kind of coaching, and once they had chased the redcoats back into their hole they proposed to sit and watch that hole. Their slogan might have been: "They shall not emerge!"

Because of their control of the waters adjacent to Boston, the British could easily have broken out anywhere, but there were two logical land exits especially to be guarded—Boston Neck and Charlestown Neck.

It was expected that the British would hold the Charlestown Peninsula, which would have been easy enough to do; and they did, just in the beginning, fortify their end of the Neck. It was expected that they would wish to prevent the Americans from taking over the tallest of the three hills, Bunker's Hill, which, in the center of this almost-island, was big enough to permit the controlling of the whole city of Boston—if there were guns enough, and powder and ball enough to feed them, and men who knew how to handle them. The British did not. They sent over an emergency squad, to keep at a distance any rebels who might try to annoy the movement of Percy's weary troops the night of the 19th and the early morning of the 20th, but soon they withdrew even these, leaving the peninsula blank, which argued, in American minds, that they were massing in the city for an attack, probably by way of Boston Neck.

Boston Neck itself was blocked by the American right wing centered at Roxbury, just south of it. The line extended from there in a northerly and westerly direction to and through Cambridge (where the bridge over the Charles had been reassembled for the second time) and on up, arching to the north, to the purlieus of Charlestown Neck. In a few days this line was extended east to Chelsea on the Mystick, making an almost perfect half-circle around the landward side of Boston. For an army that did not even have a staff this was a good arrangement.

The camp was chaotic. Men were coming and going all the time. There might have been two thousand there the first morning, and they were fed, somehow, on ship's bread originally destined for the British Navy but seized at Roxbury, and a large quantity of pork and beef earmarked for the British Army in Boston, which was never to get it. The kitchen facilities of Harvard College were used for this purpose, for Harvard, like Charlestown, like Roxbury, had been deserted by its usual residents.

More men poured in, while others, who reckoned that

they had done enough when they pursued the redcoats to cover, were picking up their muskets and—without reporting to anybody—starting home. Some, after they had straightened their affairs, would re-enlist. Others were never heard from again.

There were no tents, at first. The men as they came were bedded down anywhere—in deserted houses, in barns and stables, even corncribs, in Harvard dormitories and classrooms. There was a shortage of blankets from the beginning. Fortunately the weather was mild.

There is always a morning after. The only general officer at the American camp April 20 was still—for he had been on the job the previous night and all the previous day—tubby little William Heath. He was almost unattended and entirely unsupported as he went from place to place posting sentries, admonishing captains and lieutenants (he had to ask who these were, for there were no uniforms and no insignia of rank), collecting firewood and food, allocating sleeping quarters. One of the first orders he gave that day was to a militia company from Dedham, or rather to its captain, John Battle, "to pass over the ground which had been the scene of the action the preceding day, and to bury such of the slain as he should find unburied." He provided, among other things, to have the flour that had been retrieved from the Concord millpond brought to Cambridge, which, being the center of the line, was proclaimed headquarters.

Heath was superseded later that day by Artemas Ward of Shrewsbury, who had risen from a sickbed at dawn, a man who outranked Heath in the Massachusetts militia. Ward, forty-seven years old, was portly, florid, slow-moving, slow-speaking, serious, a somewhat Old Testament figure. The job was too much for him, but it would have been too much for any man.[17] He set up his headquarters in the Hastings house in Cambridge,[18] which was also the meeting place of the Committee of Safety, and on that very afternoon he called a council of war, the first, which consisted of himself, General

Heath, General John Whitcomb, six colonels, and six lieutenant colonels.

Ward's position was distressing. He could not command the troops to remain in camp, and he had no authority to issue "beating orders"—that is, permission to certain officers to go out into the countryside and beat a drum for enlistment purposes—which would enable him to bring in the fresh men he so badly needed.

He wrote to the Provincial Congress the fourth day of the siege: "My position is such that if I have not enlistment orders immediately, I shall be left all alone." For by that time the soldiers were departing by droves, and only coming in by dribbles. When they saw that there was no longer any fighting, and that the British were not sallying forth, the newcomers remembered that they had work to do at home, and they went away. They were willing enough to die for their country, but they saw no reason why they should just stand around doing nothing. They were not men who were accustomed to doing nothing.

The Provincial Congress gave Ward the authority he sought. This resulted, immediately, in a dearth of officers, of which there had previously been a plethora. The company officers in Cambridge, Roxbury, Chelsea, and around Prospect Hill, still all Massachusetts men, were never sure of their positions anyway ·They had not *earned* their commissions; they had not been appointed because of meritorious service; they had been elected, rather, by their own men, in accordance with the unconventional democratical system then in favor in the colony. The officers, in consequence, did not dare to be too demanding, lest the rankers elect more lenient leaders to replace them.

Such were the conditions in the tumultuous camp at Cambridge during the first days of what came to be known as the siege of Boston. Had the British struck then, the war would have been ended. The British, however, had troubles of their own.

# CHAPTER

# 11

THE FIRST EFFECT of the battle upon Boston was one of shock. It simply didn't seem possible. And when the wounded began coming in, ferried across the river from Charlestown, those in the city, military and civilian alike, were appalled.

There was no standard militia musket ball, for the guns varied in size, but a mean caliber might be .75. Such a weapon would fire a chunk of lead almost three-quarters of an inch in diameter and weighing a full ounce or even more. These, when they did not kill outright, inflicted hideous wounds, great spongy red masses scattered with spicula of smashed bone, quick to fester. The scene at the ferry was a grim one.

Tories in the town, and perhaps a few patriots as well, sent all manner of carriages and carts, and horses and servants to pull them, to the ferry house for the purpose of carrying the wounded to hastily improvised hospitals; and many female camp followers were called upon to give over their usual duties and act as nurses, being cautioned at the same time to stay sober, for they were integral members of the British Army and like their husbands or lovers could be lashed across the bare back in public.

The very day of Lexington–Concord itself, the 19th, while Boston seethed with rumors of the fighting, about 200 loyalist residents, most of them shopkeepers, had offered to fight for the British. Gage had accepted the offer with thanks, and the men were organized into a regiment of "gentlemen volunteers" under the redoubtable Timothy Ruggles, and were armed and rigorously drilled; but they were never used, and it would seem that Gage did not trust them.

Two days after the fight, April 21, Gage issued a solemn warning to Charlestown that he would burn it if there was any co-operation with the rebels. He might have saved himself the trouble. The place was empty, a ghost town. Now and then a farmer might come over from the mainland to make hay for a few hours or to tend a vegetable garden, but to all intents and purposes the whole peninsula had been deserted, the houses stripped of their furniture.

Gage did not hold Charlestown. He sent over Brigadier General Robert Pigot, a small fellow but a first-class fighting man, to relieve Lord Percy, but within a few days he withdrew Pigot and all his troops—*why* will always be one of history's mysteries.

It can be assumed that he never even thought of a sally, much less the occupation of any of the "mainland." He was waiting for reinforcements. He was the kind of general who was always waiting for reinforcements.

Early in the siege the selectmen called on General Gage and proposed that he permit all patriots who so desired to leave Boston, so that there would be fewer mouths to feed and less chance of an internal rising. He replied that this would be to give firearms to the rebels. They countered with the suggestion that nobody be allowed to depart unless and until he should have surrendered any arms he might have, and Gage agreed to this. The very next day—it was April 27—there were turned in at Faneuil Hall 1,778 muskets, 634 pistols, 973 bayonets, and 38 blunderbusses,[19] for each of which a receipt was given.

The besiegers in their turn readily agreed to allow such residents of or refugees to the hinterland to go to Boston, provided, again, that they carried no firearms. So there were switches both ways, though most of the traffic was *out* rather than *in*.

The besiegers kept their word. Gage did not. It was pointed out to him that there was inevitably a great deal of smuggling of arms, and that in any case more persons were going than were coming, so that soon Boston would contain no rebels at all, only loyalists. *Then*, it was asked, would not the rebels be tempted to burn the town? Gage saw the point. Boston was all wooden, the buildings set close together, and more often than not there was a breeze from off the bay. A fire would be a terrible thing. Also, if he kept some of the rebels he kept some hostages, though he would not use that word.

He did not issue a statement admitting that he had made a mistake. Instead, he gradually tightened the regulations, and increased the red tape, so that in a little while the law became a dead letter. There was a heap of hard feeling about this.

Combined with the affirmation that the rebels scalped their prisoners—which was almost universally believed in Boston as in the army—there was the myth, new then, of the infallibility of these misled country bumpkins as marksmen. The muster rolls—for of course the minutemen had all been paid for that famous day's work—show that a total of 3,763 members of the Massachusetts militia signed up to fight April 19, and it can be assumed that at least 3,500 of these got in at least one shot, many of them twenty or more shots. It has been estimated that about 75,000 shots were fired by the Americans, a figure that will do as well as any other. Yet the total British casualties were only 273, which works out that only about 1 in every 300 balls found a mark. However, this was considered expert shooting, as indeed it was by European standards; and it inspired fear in many a Boston breast.

There was no real suffering in Boston—none, that is, directly attributable to the siege—but there was a great deal of inconvenience. Prices went up. There was plenty to eat, but nothing fresh, all salted stuff. Fresh meat, smuggled in, sold for £1 and even £1/6 a pound, when you could get it at all. Cheese cost 15 pence to 2 shillings a pound, butter 2 shillings, bread (which formerly sold for 3 pence) a shilling a loaf, potatoes anywhere from 9 shillings to 10/6 a bushel; and there was no milk at all. The least busy member of the British Army in Boston just then was the butcher master-general, Shubael Hewes.

Moreover, there was an epidemic of smallpox. It was not a bad one, but the fact that it could not be avoided was irksome and sometimes even frightening. Previously in an epidemic of smallpox—and they were common—the well-to-do and others lucky enough to be free would get out into the country for a leisurely breather. There was no longer any going to the country for those in Boston now, whether rich or poor, and certainly not for the soldiers.

What with the wounded dying and the victims of the epidemic, so often were the passing bells tolled at the various churches—signifying the passing of a soul—that Gage, anxious about their effect upon the hearers, in an extraordinary ruling prohibited the practice.

Boston, decidedly, was not a joyous place.

# 12

OUT OF A SCOW on the western bank of Lake Champlain one dark night in May—the moon had gone down—there tumbled eighty-five men, most of them tatterdemalions in linsey-woolsey who called themselves Green Mountain Boys, though their neighbors in New York referred to them as the Bennington Mob. They were led by two extraordinary men, who walked side by side in step, each being careful that the other should not get an inch ahead of him, for each claimed to be the true and legal chief of this utterly illegal expedition.

Each of these leaders was flashy, a seeker after glory, anything but modest, and each called himself a colonel, but in personal appearance they could hardly have offered a more startling contrast.

One was tall, blond, foul-mouthed, broad of shoulder, with long arms and huge horny hands, in speech and manner the very epitome of the frontiersman, almost *flamboyantly* homespun. He was also (though it did not show this morning) a great reader, a deistic philosopher, and an author. His name was Ethan Allen, and he was, even here in life, a folk hero comparable to Hereward, Fulk FitzWarin, even Robin Hood.

The other was short, swart, a scowler, with black hair, arrogant light-gray eyes, who moved like a cat and behaved like a czar. His name was Benedict Arnold.

Arnold had recently been made a colonel of the Massachusetts militia by the Committee of Safety, with whom he had conferred after bringing a company of the Governor's

Foot Guards to the Cambridge camp from New Haven, but he still wore the uniform of a captain of that Connecticut organization—scarlet, white, and black, very smart. By trade he was a combination apothecary-merchant-bookseller, a man of many talents, who also sometimes dealt in horses and ships. He was thirty-four.

Allen wore a uniform of his own design—green coat, big gold epaulets, yellow breeches. He was thirty-seven.

The fort that they approached so silently in the darkness was Ticonderoga. It guarded the entrance of Lake George into Lake Champlain, and hence the whole water route between New York and Canada. The French had built it in 1755, laying it out along lines put down by that great master of fortification, Vauban, an imposing star-shaped structure complete with glacis, counterscarp, covered ways, and demi-lunes. In 1757, 4,000 Frenchmen under Montcalm had held it against 6,000 British regulars plus 10,000 provincial auxiliaries. It was called Fort Carillon then.

The next year, when Amherst advanced upon it, the French garrison was much smaller, and the commander, Bourlamaque, mined the whole thing and walked out. The explosion, when it occurred, pretty well blew the fort to bits. Amherst rebuilt it, though it was never again to be as strong as the original, and changed the name to Fort Ticonderoga. Since that time it had been a British Army post, though because the Treaty of Paris in 1763 had ceded Canada to Great Britain it had been allowed to deteriorate as no longer needed. It was, virtually, in ruins. But it did still house a large train of artillery, much of which might be put to use by the American people. It seemed almost certain that Whitehall soon would realize the value of Ticonderoga and cause it to be strengthened, if only to keep it out of the hands of the rebels. (In fact, orders to this effect were on their way this very morning of May 10, 1775.)

The same idea came to sundry men or groups of men at

about the same time. Local Tories advanced the possibility to the military governor of Canada, Guy Carleton, who, however, at that time did not have enough men to help them. The Green Mountain Boys looked upon it as a shrewd move, a useful pawn in their undeclared war against New York. A clique in Hartford, Connecticut, pledged that colony's money to back a venture and sent recruiters into the Green Mountain Boys' territory. This was a private thing, unauthorized. It was about to be brought off when still another party entered the proceedings—Benedict Arnold.

Captain Arnold had seen at a glance that the camp at Cambridge was no place for him. He had seen too that what it most pronouncedly lacked, aside from gunpowder, was cannon. He had heard of the train at Ticonderoga. To think, with him, was to act. He could not lead his own Foot Guard men to Lake Champlain, which was in New York, but he appealed to the Massachusetts Committee of Safety, which enthusiastically endorsed his plan, created him a colonel, and issued him beating orders to be used in western Massachusetts. He went into action immediately.

But immediately too, before he had done anything more than place his enlistment officers, he heard of the Green Mountain Boys' project. They must not get there before him! Without a musket behind him, only a single servant, he leaped on his horse and rode to Castleton in the New Hampshire Claims,[20] where he demanded that he be acknowledged as commanding officer, though the Boys had already elected Ethan Allen to this post.

They laughed at first, but when Arnold persisted there were black looks and mutterings about a necktie party, something the Green Mountain Boys were quite capable of. This did not faze Benedict Arnold, always cool in times of peril.

They began to think it over. He did have authority after all—some kind of authority—whereas they had none. This was a daring thing that they were about to do. If the colonies were to patch up their quarrel with the mother country, where would the banditti who had seized Ticonderoga be? But this Colonel Arnold, for all his stuck-up ways, *did* have a paper.

They compromised. They said that both men could lead them, together, until outside advice could be obtained.

This was why Benedict Arnold and Ethan Allen walked side by side as they approached Ticonderoga, watching each other warily, lest either dart ahead and grab the glory. There were eighty-three men behind them. There had been more than twice that many at the rendezvous on the other side of the lake, but at the last moment something had gone wrong about the boats, and it was now too late to send back for the rest: it would soon be dawn.

A sentry saw them and called a challenge, and when they made no answer he leveled his musket and pulled the trigger. He got a flash in the pan. He turned and ran inside. The Green Mountain Boys, yelling like Indians, ran after him.

Another sentry appeared, and this one had a bayonet on the end of his musket, but Colonel Allen, who had drawn his sword, knocked this aside, in the process slightly cutting the sentry's scalp—the only bloodletting on this momentous morning.

Still side by side, Arnold and Allen ran into the fort. They found themselves at the foot of a wooden stairway, and Allen waved his sword.

"*Come out, you old rat!*"

What did emerge, from a door at the head of the stair, was a young lieutenant, Jocelyn Feltham, who wore coat and waistcoat but carried his breeches in his hand. Feltham asked them what in the world they wanted, and Allen answered by demanding that he turn over to them "the fort and all the effects of George the Third." (". . . those were his words," Feltham was to remember a few days later when he wrote his report.)

In whose name, Feltham asked, were they making this demand?

*"In the name of the Great Jehovah and the Continental Congress,"* thundered Ethan Allen.

There was no resistance. The garrison, all asleep save the two sentries, consisted of Feltham and his superior, the commanding officer, Captain William Delaplace, 2 artillerymen, 2 sergeants, 44 privates, most of them old men and some of them invalids, and 24 women and children.

The next day they went a few miles north and easily took a companion but much smaller fort, Crown Point, where there were a sergeant and 8 privates, besides 10 women and children.

The total bag, besides the prisoners and the real estate, comprised 183 cannons, many of them in good condition, 19 mortars, 3 howitzers, 51 swivel guns, 52 tons of lead, and 40,000 musket cartridges.

Still acting separately, the two commanders-in-chief presented this loot to the Continental Congress assembled at Philadelphia. The Congress, scared, sent back orders that it should be taken to the southern foot of Lake George and there a careful catalogue of it should be made; but the two forts should be abandoned.[21]

For once agreeing on something, both Colonel Arnold and Colonel Allen wrote furious protests against this pusillanimity; and in time they prevailed, so that the order to abandon the forts was withdrawn.

Once started, Allen and Arnold would have gone on to invade Canada had they not been told to stay where they were. They really meant it. Carleton had only two regiments, scattered over many small posts, and these two were confidant, separately, that they could take both Montreal and Quebec and overrun the whole of Canada.

Arnold's enlistees were coming in now, and he was questioning Allen's command with more and more pertinacy, while the atmosphere at Ticonderoga grew daily more tense. A fight was averted only when the Massachusetts Committee of Safety sent a new commander-in-chief, one Benjamin Hinman, from whom Arnold was supposed to take orders. Arnold resigned in a huff, first, however, taking care to put in a big bill for expenses.

The guns stayed at Crown Point and at Ticonderoga, for the present. But they were to have a most important effect upon the siege of Boston.

CHAPTER

# 13

THAT EACH SIDE lies about losses in battle, its own and those of the enemy, is well known but not always taken into consideration; and it remains good advice to get your story told first. The Committee of Safety of the Massachusetts Provincial Congress, well aware of this, promptly after the Lexington-Concord affair appointed field workers to take depositions *in perpetuam* from survivors. The news was being spread far and wide by land, and this work the committee had well in hand by reason of the committees of correspondence previously established in every colony, and the admirable system of dispatch riders. Though time was needed —word of the battle did not reach Charleston, South Carolina, until May 10, the very day the Continental Congress called itself to order in Philadelphia, the day that Ticonderoga was taken, almost a month after the event, and that was esteemed excellent time—the patriots could be sure that only *their* tale was told.

It was even more important to get to England with that news before General Gage did. The Massachusetts Congress, a few days later, elected Dr. Warren its president, and it was probably he—for Sam Adams was in Philadelphia—who wrote the Continental report, a masterpiece of propaganda. Gage actually got his report off a few days before the patriots were ready with their own, but they had troubled themselves to charter a very fast vessel, which got there well ahead of the other. The news in England caused a tremendous sensation; and by the time Gage's official report came along—and it was a dull document at best—it sounded lame, halting, apologetic.

Englishmen by and large were dismayed by the prospect of another war: they were still paying through the nose for the last one. King George, however, did not seem to sense this. The king was really ruling, not just reigning, and he was determined to see that his dignity was upheld across the sea. Massive preparations for the shipment of supplies and reinforcements to America were being made, so that it jolted no one, though it amused some, when no fewer than three major generals were sent off for those shores at one time—and in a vessel called *Cerberus*. A wit picked this up:

> "Behold the Cerberus the Atlantic plow,
> Her precious cargo—Burgoyne, Clinton, Howe.
> Bow, wow, wow!"

That, however, was before the arrival of the statement Dr. Warren had written. Afterward it was as though nothing from or about America would ever seem funny again.

May 5 the Provincial Congress adopted a resolution declaring that General Gage had "utterly disqualified himself to serve this colony as governor, and in every other capacity; and that no obedience ought, in future, to be paid, by the several towns and districts in this colony, to his writs for calling an assembly, or to his proclamations, or any other of his acts or doings; but that, on the other hand, he ought to be considered and guarded against, as an unnatural and inveterate enemy to this country."[22] This altered nothing.

As early as May 3 the Provincial Congress had suggested to the Continental Congress, informally, that a federal army be formed; and May 12 it drafted an appeal to that effect, which appeal was ready four days later and was sent to Philadelphia by that unwavering patriot Dr. Benjamin Church.

May 6 four companies of the 65th infantry regiment came from Halifax, joining the two companies that were already in Boston. May 14 the first of what were to be 600 marines arrived, and the rest came May 23. May 25 the three major generals themselves put in, and there was much ado indeed.

William Howe, the senior in rank, was a large slow sleepy man with a dark complexion and a gentle voice, no barker. He liked his liquor as he liked his women, raw. He would sit up gambling night after night. He was never in a hurry. Yet he had written a book on infantry tactics and he had led the van up to the Plains of Abraham on the famous day when Wolfe met Montcalm and won Canada, a battle in which William Howe had covered himself with glory.

Henry Clinton was a ramrod with damn-you eyes, very positive in everything that he said, though less so in what he did, a sort of eighteenth-century Colonel Blimp. He was a career man, having been in the service since the age of thirteen, and he was a stickler for regulations, a man who would take no nonsense from anybody. His handwriting was execrable, his spelling worse, but this did not bother one who was aristocratic enough to rise above grammar.

John ("Gentleman Johnny") Burgoyne at fifty-three was dapper, dashing, a bit of a peacock. He was married to a daughter of Earl Derby, and David Garrick had just pro-duced his play, *Maid of the Oaks*. He believed—and in this he was unique among British generals—that the rank and file should be treated as men, not as beasts. In Parliament (all three of these personages were members of the House of Commons) he had called America a spoiled child but had said that he would rather see her convinced by persuasion than by the sword. His military record was brilliant. He had not joined the army until he was twenty-two, and though he was the oldest of the three in years he was the third in rank, in seniority. Burgoyne it was, who, after learning of the siege from a pilot in Boston Bay, cried: "What! Ten thousand peasants keeping five thousand of the King's men captive? Well, let *us* in and we'll soon make elbow-room." He was

GENERAL JOHN BURGOYNE

never allowed to forget that crack. General Elbow-Room he was to be called in his captivity.

"As our generals have now arrived," Lord Percy wrote to a friend at home, "I take it for granted that something will be undertaken."[23]

Many others took this for granted as well, including those outside Boston, but all, like the noble lord himself, were mistaken.

This was not the fault of the newly arrived generals, who were full of helpful advice. Boston, they saw right away, was not the port that Great Britain should hold. Boston offered nothing, and though it was easily defended it could be rendered harmless—as was being proved—by a gang of bumpkins. Boston was the place first appointed to be punished, it was true; but the rebellion since that time had leaped the city lines, as Lexington-Concord showed, and now it had spread everywhere. A larger plan must be made, Howe and Clinton declared.

Clinton was all for an amphibious descent upon Rhode Island, perhaps Newport itself for a starter but eventually the whole Narragansett Bay region. Rhode Island needed punishment too: had they forgotten the burning of the *Gaspee?* The hinterland there was at least as productive as that behind Boston, and from Newport British naval vessels could control all of Long Island Sound, all of the rich Connecticut shoreline; from there, too, if it seemed advisable, they could blockade New York City.

It was New York City that Howe wanted to take, deserting dreary Boston. New York, after all, controlled the Hudson River and by means of that the whole water route to Canada (he had not yet heard about the taking of Ticonderoga). New York would be easily defended, and you could cut the provinces in half. Only the New England colonies, General Howe contended, were really interested in independence; and the New England colonies in themselves could be readily subdued. Without their incitement the middle and southern colonies would see the light and would return to their proper allegiance to His Gracious Majesty the King. That was William Howe's advice—take New York.

Thomas Gage listened to them both; listened carefully and long; and did nothing.

As for John Burgoyne, he was looking after John Burgoyne. It needed no exposition to demonstrate to him that there was not a future for his talents in these provincial purlieus. Gage would be recalled soon, true; that much was an open secret; but two generals who outranked Burgoyne would still remain, and each of them younger than he. Whether they went to Newport or to New York, or stayed here, he would be overshadowed, unappreciated. An independent command was what he wanted, so that he could expand.

A man should take advantage of a war; and Burgoyne had plenty of confidence in himself.

He also had plenty of friends in high political places, and he would write to them. From the beginning he had put his pen at the service of his commander, and had become a sort of literary ghost for General Gage, who himself was not much of a hand at writing. But there was other, less public work to be done. A prodigious puller of wires, even though they might be 3,000 miles long, Gentleman Johnny settled down to get himself a better post.

Meanwhile, outside the city that same rabble of farmers, blacksmiths, shopkeepers, milled around as before, falling over one another, but all the time keeping an eye on that hole down which the foe had dropped.

# 14

THE ANCIENT CUSTOM of allowing for a large number of women camp followers when an army takes the field, a custom continued by the British right into the last quarter of the eighteenth century, never did gain recognition among the Americans, who would have regarded such women, with horror, as harlots.

In the British Army they were not necessarily that. In theory at least they were the wives of sergeants and privates, and some may indeed have been married: certainly they had children from time to time, which complicated matters. "Camp followers" sounds like hangers-on, parasites; but in the British Army they were an integral part of a given force, calculated, as were the men, by regiments. They were not paid, but they were allotted half a ration of food, their small children a quarter ration each. Provision was made for transporting them and for sheltering them in camp. They were not a horde, a loose amorphous mass, as in the old days—the Duke of Alva when in 1567 he marched to conquer the Low Countries for Philip II of Spain had 10,000 men accompanied by 2,000 female camp followers, every one registered—but on the contrary their numbers were sharply limited, not by custom but rather by the taste of the commanding officer. At Crown Point the women and children actually outnumbered the men; at Quebec there was one camp follower to every thirteen soldiers, a high percentage; Braddock took scores of them when he started for a Fort Duquesne he was never to reach; and when all reinforcements had been landed in Boston

—for none of these women were local talent, they were all brought in—there were about 650 of them.[24]

They were a drab, sleazy lot, as far as it is possible to conceive from their sisters of the world of hoopskirts, pomatum, furbelows, and flirting fans, more filthy of speech, if such were possible, than the men they served. They were most characteristic when they jeered and spat upon prisoners of war, using language that might cause even a trooper to blush. They thieved, they quarreled, and caused fights among the men. Worst of all, they smuggled in spirits.

"Drunk for a penny, dead drunk for two," read the signs before many a city doorway in England, not so long ago; and it was sometimes added that the straw on which to sleep it off would be thrown in free. The Gin Act of 1736 and sundry subsequent and related pieces of legislation, requiring a license fee from the proprietor and thereby raising the price of the liquor, had somewhat helped to better these conditions; but still, it remained the tendency of the English lower classes to stupefy themselves with strong drink whenever opportunity offered, a privilege that once had been confined to their betters. Boston, from this point of view, was a paradise. Even in the middle of the siege, sixpence would get you a full quart of West Indian rum, fourpence a quart of the local product— *if* you could find a camp follower to smuggle it in to you.

The female camp followers were sometimes used as nurses, in emergencies, as after the Lexington-Concord battle, but most of the time this work was done by men. The women's chief function, aside from whatever private ones they might care to perform—their *raison d'être* as far as the Army was concerned—was to take in washing and mend the men's clothes. Here was no easy task. Above all the Army insisted upon "smartness." Every button must be polished (the buttons were all metal: the soldiers scornfully called civilians "mohairs" because they used cloth buttons), every belt pipeclayed, every wig powdered, every boot made to look like a black mirror, all the time. Shirts must be spotless, neckpieces too.

In the American camp there was a shortage of soap, but the chief reason for its disgusting dirtiness was the absence of women. That dirtiness was commented upon by every visitor. It was not until two weeks after the camp had been laid out that the men even began to dig latrines: until that time they had gone just anywhere. Drinking did not pose a problem— the men were issued half a gill of rum or a quart of spruce beer or cider each day, when there was any on hand—but dirt, decidedly, did.

A place of garbage the camp at Cambridge might be. A place of sin it was not. Just occasionally a parsonic visitor might be shocked by some of the language he heard, but not often; and as military encampments went it was downright chaste. There was a large admixture of parsons among the men themselves, and they were not marked off by any sort of clerical garb, as they would be in England. That man next to you, the one cleaning his gun, might be a preacher. The whole settlement had, in fact, a somewhat *camp-meetingy* air. So many of the men had Old Testament names: Nehemiahs, Ezekiels, Jabezes, Amoses, Moseses, Aarons, Calebs abounded, and there was more than a smattering of Sennacheribs, Epaphrodituses, and Nebuchadnezzars. In ordinary conversation General Gage was often referred to as Pharaoh, or perhaps the Anti-Christ, the redcoats as the Philistines, the Americans themselves as the Chosen People. It was still one hundred percent a New England aggregation, with representatives from no other colonies, not even New York, strictly Yankee, and there were prayer meetings every morning, while preachings, whether professional or laic, were likely to occur at any hour. Debates about the Gospels and Original Sin were common, on duty or off.

Men like that would never consent to the presence of female camp followers even if such could be found in America. They would rather stay dirty.

# 15

THE APPEARANCE of the camp reflected its confusion, its makeshiftness. There were no flags. Drums were sometimes heard, never a bugle. The men were divided into companies and regiments, but there were no brigades or divisions, and the regiments and companies were of many different sizes. Here and there was a spot of colorful uniform, where some such spruce semi-private outfit as the Connecticut Governor's Foot Guards[25] or John Chester's Wethersfield company strutted; but in general it was impossible to tell the officers from the men, except that some of the officers did wear swords. There was precious little saluting.

There *was* excitement. Again and again the word would go out that the British were about to come forth and attack, and there would be a shouting of orders, a flurry of muskets, a hurrying to breastworks. One of the worst of these was April 24, just a few days after the battle, and because this was the festival of St. George it seemed almost certain that the British would attack; but they did not. May 9 there was a similar scare.

Artemas Ward continued to work closely with the Committee of Safety, sharing the same headquarters building. The Committee in its turn worked well with the Provincial Congress, which met in almost continuous session in nearby Watertown. It would sometimes get answers back from the parent body in a few hours, but when it thought that time pressed it did not hesitate to act on its own. Mindful of the Praetorian Guard, not forgetting Oliver Cromwell either, the

Committee of Safety was scrupulously careful to keep itself superior to the military arm, an attitude that suited Ward very well, for he had no thought of seizing the reins of government.

It was hard to get the coastal towns to contribute recruits, for they feared the British Navy much more than they feared the British Army, and with reason; and far from sending men to Cambridge most of them kept up a continuous clamor for militiamen to be sent to *them*. Nevertheless, once the preliminary fuss was over, the New England colonies, though they did not meet the quotas they had set for themselves, did send large bodies of militiamen to Cambridge. These men, most of them, had signed up for the rest of the year. Nobody thought that the war was going to last long.

The New Hampshire contingent of 1,200 under John Stark was one of the first in the field. They had orders to put themselves under the command of Artemas Ward for the present, though this of course was only a favor and could be withdrawn at any time.

The Rhode Island contribution of 1,000, if the smallest, was the best equipped. It did not have uniforms, but it did have its own tents, which were not a higgledy-piggledy of sizes, shapes, and colors, like the others in the camp, but all alike. The Rhode Islanders were in charge of a slow-spoken ex-Quaker named Nathanael Greene, who was a natural soldier. Artemas Ward's orders of the day were circulated among them, but they obeyed only when they felt like obeying; for why should they listen to a Massachusetts man?

Massachusetts itself, by far the most populous of the colonies (it included Maine then), was supposed to maintain 11,500 men in the field.

Connecticut's quota was 2,300, and though these men were fussy about taking orders from any but their own hand-picked officers, in general they did consent to let Ward at least have the last word. The Connecticut men were under

ISRAEL "OLD PUT" PUTNAM

Israel Putnam, another legend-in-his-own-lifetime, a rolypoly red-faced veteran of the French and Indian War about whom tremendously tall tales were told. Putnam was fifty-seven—Old Put they called him—but he could bustle about like a boy, and did. He believed in keeping others busy as well, and he was soon building breastworks, rather pretentiously called forts, in and near Cambridge. "It is better to dig a ditch every morning and fill it up at night than to have the men idle," he used to say; and: "Your Yankee is a funny creature. He likes to have his legs covered. Put him *behind* something and he'll fight all day." Old Put was usually active in the various chase-aways when the British tried to carry off hay or cattle or sheep from the various islands in Boston Bay—Noddle's, Snake, Hog, Grape.[26]

Boston, itself a peninsula, was guarded by or threatened by two other peninsulas—Charlestown to the northwest,

Dorchester (it was then called Dorchester Neck—not the Neck that led to it but the whole peninsula) to the southeast. From the highest hill on each of these—Nook's Hill in the northwestern part of Dorchester, Bunker's Hill in the middle of Charlestown—the whole city, as well as the ships in the bay, could be swept by cannon fire. Yet both peninsulas were deserted, untouched.

May 12 the Committee of Safety and Council of War (as it was then called, and as in fact it *was*) recommended that fortifications be built on all approaches to Charlestown Neck. These assumedly would have been for the purpose of preventing the British from occupying the peninsula and then sallying forth into the countryside. Prospect Hill and Winter Hill must have been meant, though they were not mentioned by name. Between them, together with the smaller Plowed Hill, they controlled the narrow entrance of the Neck.

The recommendation went on to call for "a strong Redoubt raised on Bunker's Hill, with cannon planted there." This was easy to write, but naïve. Did the committeemen really think that the British in Boston would stand by and watch such a move made? Or were they *looking* for a fight?

The very next day the ebullient Putnam gathered around him all of the men of the center, Cambridge and its environs, who were not on sentry duty or some work detail, a little over 2,000 of them, and he marched these across Charlestown Neck. On what authority he did this nobody, including himself, seemed to know. He marched them over Bunker's Hill and then over the lesser Breed's Hill, which was nearer Boston, and so into the village of Charlestown itself. There he placed them with their backs against the empty houses, along the waterfront, and encouraged them in some indiscriminate and seemingly aimless warwhooping, while the gunners of the nearby frigate *Somerset* watched with pitying grins, thinking how easy it would be to knock these buffoons to Kingdom Come.

Afterward, having done nothing else, Israel Putnam led the men back to their camp.

It could hardly be called a reconnaissance in force, for such was not needed: there were many men in the American camp who knew every square inch of the Charlestown Peninsula. It was rather a demonstration of exuberance. It was also good exercise.

June 6 two significant events took place, one to the north of Boston, the other to the south.

About noon of that day Old Put and Dr. Warren, together with certain wounded British marines, and escorted by the swank Wethersfield company, proceeded to the village of Charlestown, where by prearrangement they met a Major Moncrief, an admirer of Old Put from the French and Indian War days, and a lieutenant of marines, who was in charge of sundry patriot prisoners to be exchanged. Dr. Warren and the officers had a friendly drink in the home of Dr. Foster, one room of which had been dressed for the occasion, and everything went swimmingly. This exchange is remarkable as indicating that the British were beginning to take the war seriously and also that they were learning that Americans could sometimes act like gentlemen.

At the same time, to the south, generals Ward, Thomas, Spencer, and Heath, accompanied by some lesser officers, made a careful, unhurried inspection of the Dorchester Peninsula. What did this portend? The British fired at them from the battery on Boston Neck, doubtless expecting them to scatter in panic, but this did nothing to disturb the inspection.

A few days later—it was June 12—General Gage issued what was surely one of the most pompous and meaningless official papers ever to come from a colonial governor's desk, polysyllabic to the point of preposterousness, a paper that read as though it was meant to be a burlesque of the period's most fulsome prose. It was, of course, the work of Gentleman Johnny Burgoyne.

Abigail Adams, in a letter to her husband John, who was in Philadelphia, found it reprehensible. "All the records of time cannot produce a blacker page. Satan, when driven from the regions of bliss, exhibited not more malice. Surely the father of lies is superseded."[27] In London the journalists, like most Americans, did not take the proclamation so seriously. Rather they roared with laughter at: "The authors of the present unnatural revolt have uniformly placed their chief confidence in the suppression of truth . . . The press has been invariably prostituted . . . till, to complete the horrid profanation of terms and ideas, the name of God has been introduced in the pulpits, to excite and justify devastation and massacre." This was silly enough, in all truth, but what chiefly tickled the risibilities of the Londoners was the assertion that the rude rebels "with a preposterous parade of military arrangement affected to hold the Army besieged." *That*, in the circumstances, was really rich.

The proclamation, almost incidentally, invoked martial law. It also offered pardon to all who would immediately lay down their arms, excepting always those arch-traitors, Samuel Adams and John Hancock. It had no effect whatever, after the laugh.

The next day word came to the headquarters in Cambridge, through reliable spies, that the British were making preparations to take over the whole Dorchester Peninsula on the 18th (that it would be the Lord's Day shows what sort of people they were over there). This was serious. Something had to be done.

# 16

O<small>F STUDENTS</small> at Harvard, *as* students, there were none left; but the president of the college, the Reverend Samuel Langdon, had stuck to his post. The Reverend Mr. Langdon was known for his long sermons, and when he appeared before about 1,000 Massachusetts militiamen on the common at Cambridge just after sundown, Thursday, June 15, they knew that they were to hear something special. Respectfully they doffed their hats.

The sky was washed with stars, but the night was dark, for the moon, waning, was a mere silver sliver low over the western horizon. It was dry, and not cold.

The Reverend Mr. Langdon invoked the blessing of God upon the task they were about to undertake, and at great length he adjured them to be firm and courageous in the performance of that task, but he did not say what the task *was*. It may be that he didn't know. The men did not know, though they must have smelled something unusual in the air, for they had been kept busy all afternoon with hand molds molding musket balls from great chunks of lead. (In the British Army this work could be done in vast quantities, since the Brown Bess was a standard weapon, but with the Americans it was each man for himself, according to the caliber of his musket barrel.)

When the sermon was over at last they donned their hats again and fell in behind their officers and started northeast, all without a sound. Two sergeants led the way, and they held bull's-eye lanterns with the backs open.

When they came to Charlestown Neck, where they were

halted for a little while, they believed that they knew where they were going, and they started to discuss this move, though in low voices. In an ordinary army the soldiers would not be permitted to argue for or against the judgment of their generals; but this was not an ordinary army. The generals themselves had been talking about it for several days. John Thomas, the quiet-spoken physician who was commander of the right wing at Roxbury, was emphatically against any occupation of Charlestown Peninsula, for he thought that this might tend to weaken his own wing in defense of Boston Neck, the point from which he and so many others expected an attack. Artemas Ward was by no means enthusiastic. It was Israel Putnam who, very largely single-handed, had won a grudging consent for the Charlestown move. Putnam was there that night, but though as a brigadier he was the highest ranking officer, he was not in charge. The Massachusetts men liked him personally, but after all he came from Connecticut. The commanding officer, by appointment of the Committee of Safety, was another farmer, William Prescott of Pepperell.

Prescott was a veteran of the French and Indian War, a tall dour thin man in homespun, with light-brown hair which was rather long, but bald on top. Tonight he wore a floppy black felt hat, and a banyan, a light, loose, light-brown duster or coat. He carried a sword, which he knew how to use. He was a man who never raised his voice, a man in whom anybody would have confidence.

They were joined, near the entrance to the Neck, by some wagons filled with entrenching tools, after which there was no doubt about the intention of fortifying the peninsula.

Those who were against the plan said that it would be too easy for the British to stop all reinforcements and supplies by means of a bombardment of the Neck. They could not land troops on the Neck itself, because of the presence of a large shallow mill dam, but they could land troops *near* the Neck, pinching off the whole peninsula; and after that it would be a simple matter to starve the patriots into submission.[28]

Those who were in favor of the plan said that it was time *somebody* did *something;* that the men were going stale from inaction.

At this same point they were also joined by about 200 men from the nearby Connecticut encampment. These were not in direct charge of Old Put, who, on a horse, was here, there, and elsewhere, but of Captain Thomas Knowlton, a dashing young officer who was personally against the plan but was not the sort to be left out of a fight.[29]

They got over the Neck all right, and then the leaders—Prescott, Putnam, Colonel Richard Gridley, the chief engineer, and some others—went into a huddled conference on the shore of the Charles, while the rank and file, once again, waited, doing nothing.

The order was clear enough, and in writing. They had it there. It stipulated that "possession of the hill called Bunker's Hill, in Charlestown, be securely kept and defended; and also, some one hill or hills on Dorchester Neck be likewise secured . . . that the above mentioned Bunker's Hill be maintained, by sufficient forces being posted there. . . ."[30] Here was a large order; but the present force was concerned only with the first part of it.

There were three hills in Charlestown. On the river, directly across from Boston, was Moulton's Hill, only 35 feet high; it was never considered. Behind that, away from Boston, nearer the center of the peninsula, was Breed's Hill, 75 feet high. North and west of this, and connected with it by a high spiny ridge, was the 110-foot Bunker's Hill, named after John Bunker, a Scottish farmer who had come over in 1634, one of the first settlers, and had done well.

Breed's Hill was sometimes thought of and referred to as a part of Bunker's Hill, and indeed the name Bunker's Hill not infrequently was used to indicate the whole peninsula. It could hardly be supposed that the members of the Committee of Safety expected so slim a force to fortify and hold the entire peninsula. The point the men on the banks of the

Charles were arguing was: Granted that the real Bunker's Hill was the ultimate objective, would it be better to take it first and take Breed's Hill later if there was still time, or the other way 'round?

The order had been issued by the Committee three days before, and these leaders were all familiar with the terrain, so it might be taken for granted that they would have threshed the thing out in advance. As it was, and while the men waited, doing nothing, the better part of two precious hours was wasted.

At last they started forward, still in silence. The wisp of a moon had disappeared, and the night was warm and virtually breezeless.

They skirted the steep-sided Bunker's and climbed to the top of Breed's. There, moving swiftly, they laid out a pattern and began to dig.

This would be, technically, a redoubt—that is, an earth-work fort. It was square, a little over 130 feet on each side. The walls were of varying heights and thicknesses, the strongest being the side toward Boston, which side was additionally protected by a V-shaped outjutting known as a redan. The "back" of the redoubt, the side facing Bunker's Hill, was largely open.

The men would work for a few hours, then stand sentry for an hour, then work again. Repeatedly, silence was enjoined of them. Even the people of Boston might hear the click of a pick against rock, if they listened hard enough. It was not this that was feared. It was the war vessels.

*Lively*, a 20-gun sloop, the smallest, was near the navy yard; the brig *Somerset*, flagship of the fleet, with 68 guns, was anchored at the ferry house on the far side of the Charles; the 24-gun *Glasgow* was near Craig's Bridge; the armed transports *Symmetry* and *Cerberus* were close at hand, and off Moulton's Point was *Falcon*. These were all closer-in than any Boston house.

The sound of the sundry ship's bells, rung every half hour, came clearly to the men who toiled atop Breed's Hill, as did too the "All's well" with which their sentries saluted one another from time to time.

Prescott sent a small party, about ten men under Captain John Nutting, to the village, and he sent Captain Hugh Maxwell with a similar squad down to the shore near the ferry, the point nearest Boston. These men were admonished, especially, to listen. Prescott himself, in the company of Major John Brooks, went down there more than once to check the patrols.

In the wagons that had brought the entrenching tools—which wagons, with the horses, had immediately after unloading returned to Cambridge—were also bundles of sticks tied together and canvas or linen bags to be filled on the spot as needed with stones and dirt. These were called, respectively, fascines and gabions. Unless there was a grizzled veteran or two of the siege of Louisbourg it is not likely that any of the Americans had ever seen these devices, or even heard of them, though they were common equipment in European armies, professional armies. They helped greatly in the building of the breastworks, saving time.

So it went—moiling, mucking, inglorious work. But the job was done by dawn.

Somebody aboard the *Lively* was the first so see the miracle—a full-fledged fort on the top of a hill where the night before there had been no fort at all. He called the captain, who tumbled out of his bunk.

The captain too could hardly believe his eyes. But he wasted no time. He ordered his men to battle stations, put a spring in his cable and caused the vessel to be worn around so that she was broadside-to, and he opened up with everything he had.

The battle had begun.

# 17

For hundreds of years cannons had been used only in ships and in siege warfare, being much too heavy and hard to handle for work in the field. Lately, however, improvements in the metal and in the gunpowder had made lighter pieces practicable, and the artillery arm came into being vis-à-vis the infantry. For the first time iron balls were being fired not just at ships and at walls but at *men*. Moreover, a musket would do well if it carried 100 yards, but a light fieldpiece could carry four to five times that distance.

What cannon could do when directed against courageous but untrained men had been demonstrated more than once—recently, for example, against the followers of the Young Pretender in 1745–46, when the doughty Highlanders, who would charge anything else made by man or God, flinched and broke when confronted with "the mother of muskets." It was demonstrated yet again on the day of Lexington and Concord, when Lord Percy, whose men, in his own words, were "under an incessant fire, which like a moving circle surrounded and followed us wherever we went," might well have lost his whole force had he not paused now and then to cause his two 6-pounders to cough.[31] That invariably made the minutemen scatter, and even retreat a little.

*Lively*'s cocky little attack soon ceased, doubtless on orders from the admiral, who would need time and some breakfast in order to learn what the devil had happened; but there was no doubt that it would soon start again, and not just one vessel but all of them. This was what the Yankee leaders feared. Would the men take it?

The British superiority in cannon, June 16 on and near

the Charlestown Peninsula, was massive. The Americans had four badly handled little 4-pounders, lately seized from a British sloop and mounted on temporary carriages, which came late and left early. As against this the British had their guns guarding Boston Neck, some of them very big ones; their huge artillery park in the city proper; the guns of the fleet, almost 200 in number; two shallow-draft floating batteries, each with two 12-pounders, which had been worked in close to threaten Charlestown Neck; and four 24-pounders mounted on Copp's Hill in Boston, an eminence equal to that of Breed's Hill itself, at which it could shoot straight-across.

Also, the British had all but unlimited stocks of powder, which was in exceedingly short supply in the American camp.[32]

The peninsula was a little more than a mile long, a little less than a mile across at the widest part, the base. The eastern portion was largely hayfields and pastures, the western largely orchards and vegetable gardens. Just east of Breed's Hill there were some old clay pits and brick kilns, and to the north and east alike there was a lot of sloughy ground. As part of the overall plan, outside of the redoubt itself, as a protection for the left wing, three small flèches[33] had been dug—triangular earthen outworks with no roofs, open at the back, much like redans or ravelins—but with the coming of dawn it was seen that these would not be enough. The Mystick, so near Boston Bay, was a tidal river, and at low tide there would be plenty of room in that direction for the enemy to make a flanking movement beyond musket range from either the redoubt itself or any of the flèches. That must never be permitted. Thomas Knowlton and his Connecticut militiamen were sent down there to man and as much as possible to strengthen a low stone wall about 200 yards long that ran almost to but not quite to the water. The bombardment had been recommenced, and not just by the *Lively* but by all the vessels and the Copp's Hill battery as well, but Knowlton's men, comfortably out of reach, did not worry about this.

They had found that the stone wall was crisscrossed with wooden rails, and they gathered armfuls of the new-mown hay that lay in windrows all around and piled this into the V's of the rails, in the hope of making the structure look more formidable. The hay, fortunately, still was green: otherwise it might have caught fire from their muskets when the time came to fight.

It was going to be a hot day, that was clear.

Prescott had a conference with his officers. Most of them were in favor of asking for relief: the men had been up all night, working hard, and they were tired. No, said Prescott. The men would fight harder for what they themselves had built. However, he did agree to ask for reinforcements, and Major Brooks was told off to go and fetch them. Brooks asked the officers of the artillery unit for the loan of a horse (Colonel Gridley himself, a middle-aged man, was ill and had returned to Cambridge), but they would not grant it. They considered themselves, as artillerists, superior to mere infantrymen: it was a common attitude of the time. They might need all the horses to pull the guns away, they pointed out. So Major Brooks had to walk. The distance was a little over four miles, each way.

The balls—and the air was full of them now, and the noise was terrific—either flew overhead, or, more often, thudded into the side of the hill. Very few came into the redoubt, and then only because they had rolled up the side of the hill. The men had finished the earthworks proper and were constructing a fire step, so that they were safe enough as long as they kept their heads down.

One of them failed to do this, and he died messily, a tangle of blood and bone. It scared many of the men, who ceased work and gathered around, goggle-eyed. This was their first casualty.

"Who was he?" asked Colonel Prescott.

"Asa Pollard of Jonathan Stickney's Billerica company," an aide replied. "What shall we do with him?"

"Bury him."

"What! Without any prayers?"

The aide was right. There is nothing so disheartening to a soldier as the gory corpse of one of his companions, and already some of the men were edging toward the back of the redoubt, wondering if they could slip away; but there was a preacher near at hand—there always was—and Prescott, who knew his Yankees, was persuaded to permit a short service at the grave.

Still, the men were edgy. Old Put Putnam had taken command—by whose authority it was not clear—on Bunker's Hill itself, where he meant to dig in; and he sent to the redoubt to ask for the entrenching tools as fast as the men there were finished with them. Prescott demurred. The men he might send with the tools across that spiny ridge to Bunker's, he predicted, would never come back. Old Put vowed that he would see to it personally that they did; and at last Prescott consented. But Prescott had been right. Very few of the men returned.[34]

Both figuratively and literally—for the sun was furious now—that redoubt soon was going to be a very hot place.

Prescott climbed to the top of the breastwork. This was a perilous thing to do, for though most of the balls flew high through the air or else plopped thuddingly into the hill itself—*Falcon* and *Lively*, which had shifted her position, were pounding the hill, *Somerset* was slamming the land just above the ferry landing, the two floating batteries and the *Glasgow* and *Symmetry* were concentrating on the Neck—still, the big 24-pounders on Copp's Hill, immediately across the river, were speaking constantly, and they could and just might reach him. He ignored them, for he was intent upon restoring confidence to the men. He strolled as if through a summer garden, calling encouragement, making solemn jokes, displaying never a twitch of nervousness.

He was careful not to look anxiously toward Boston, but he must have been aware, from stolen glances, that a great deal was going on in the city. Troopers were tumbling out of their tents, and being paraded on the common, and marching in serried ranks toward the Long Wharf, where barges were being assembled. Did this mean that they were about to cross the Charles and storm the Breed's Hill redoubt? or was it a feint calculated to make the Yankees deduce *just* that move, and did it precede a grand breakout at Boston Neck while the rebels' army was so sadly split?

It was the latter possibility—that the British might be maneuvering for a Boston Neck plunge—that Artemas Ward at headquarters had to keep in mind. Appealed to by Major Brooks, at first he was reluctant to part with more than a third of John Stark's New Hampshire command, though when pleaded with he at last consented to commit it all and all of Reed's New Hampshire regiment as well. These were encamped conveniently near Charlestown Neck, which they were now ordered to cross. But that was all of the men under his command that Ward thought he should release. He had to keep his right wing strong at all costs.

Putnam, less conservative, ordered out the smart Wethersfield company of Connecticut men.

In lovely old Province House in Boston, the Governor's residence, there had been an important conference soon after dawn, and now there was to be a second one.

Admiral Graves had seen that the emergency was real, and he had ordered that not only should *Lively* resume firing but all of the other vessels should hammer away at the rebels.

William Howe, who as ranking major general would surely be in charge of any force that might be sent across the Charles, had cut his conference attendance short to go out in a rowboat on a reconnaissance trip. From midstream in the Mystick, he now reported, he had seen that the rebels' left wing, along that bank, was virtually unprotected. It should be an easy matter, and comparatively bloodless, to threaten the front of the redoubt with a large force while hooking around to the right, the *British* right, and getting behind that redoubt, the back of which probably was not protected at all: the rebels could not possibly have done all *that* work in one night. The redcoats would then have the rebels between two fires, without ever having got within range of their muskets, Howe said.

General Clinton, the bluff, pointed to a map. Would it not be easiest, he asked, to pinch off the whole peninsula by seizing Charlestown Neck?

General Gage shook his head. That would be to put a force between two enemy forces, he pontificated, which was contrary to good standard military procedure. Gage was right, by the textbooks. A more imaginative commander might have divined that the enemy could not possibly lift their guard at Boston Neck in order to plug the "mainland" side of Charlestown Neck.

General Howe was ordered to go ahead with his feint-in-front-and-encircle-with-the-right-wing plan, and General Clinton was instructed to hold himself in readiness to fly to Howe's support if needed.

As for General Burgoyne, he was given charge of the battery on Copp's Hill, a lusterless and very noisy post for a dashing cavalry officer, but it did give him an unparalleled view of the spectacle that was about to unfold.

Now Gage was gazing through a glass at a lank brown-clad figure who strode the top of the breastwork high up there on the top of Breed's Hill. He lowered the glass, and passed it to the provincial chancellor, a lawyer, Abijah Willard.

"Who is that man up there? D'ye know him?"

Abijah looked, and a small thorny smile touched his mouth.

"Aye, I know him. His name is Prescott, and he happens to be my brother-in-law."

"Will he fight?"

Abijah handed back the glass.

"Sir, I don't know about the men under him, but—*William Prescott will fight you to the gates of hell!*"

Gage pondered this for a moment, then said:

"The works must be taken."

# 18

There was never a battle with such an audience. At the first crash of cannon thousands in Boston and the surrounding towns tumbled out of bed and climbed up on something or out on something to see the pageant. The roofs were black with spectators.

Here was storybook warfare, warfare as it ought to be, with banners and bright colors, with all the brave accouterments, upon which the sun shone brightly.

The British barges began to cross at about half-past one, twenty-eight of them, in two parallel columns of fourteen each, the oars swinging rhythmically (they were handled by navy men, not soldiers) and glittering in the sun. There were forty-odd redcoats in each barge, and in some were small, toylike, brass 6-pounders.

Regimental flags fluttered over them—the 5th, the 52nd, the 38th, the 43rd.

All the while the cannons boomed, so that the landing should not be contested, and grayish smoke drifted across the bay.

Most of the spectators assumed that the landing would be at the village of Charlestown, the southernmost part of the peninsula, the nearest port to Boston; but Howe feared that a few determined companies of irregulars in the deserted town could cause trouble and might even bring about a delaying house-to-house action (in fact, Nutting and Maxwell and their men had been recalled to the main body, but Howe could not know this). Moulton's Point, just below Moulton's Hill, was picked instead, an excellent landing site with a wide and shallow beach. There the redcoats scrambled ashore with their muskets and their big black knapsacks, and formed up in file.

The barges immediately put back for more, still keeping perfect order.

The second batch contained, besides more redcoats, many men in the dark blue coats of the royal artillery. They also contained Major General William Howe and his staff.

This made a total of 1,550, the sum Howe had stipulated in his first plan. However, while he crossed, the general had noted churning masses of men farther back, on Bunker's Hill, so that he supposed that the rebels were bringing up huge reserves. He saw more. He saw some of those men, a comparatively orderly body of them, start down toward the banks of the Mystick, marching well until they were lost to his sight by reason of Moulton's Hill.

So the rebels were stiffening their left wing? When Howe had examined that neighborhood early in the morning from a boat in the river, he had seen nothing that would seem to make it defensible—only a scattering of low stone walls. Yet these peasants surely would not dream of meeting an attack by British regulars unless and until they had something to hide behind, and already they had shown an uncanny ability to make fortifications appear where a little earlier no fortifications had been. This would not be the walk-around the general had plotted.

He told his men to lug out their rations and treat themselves to some lunch, and he sent back to Boston for reinforcements. He had always been one to take his time.

In the redoubt the men, their work done, and being hot, hungry, tired, thirsty, and not unafraid, were silent; there was nothing for them to do now but wait. Behind them, on Bunker's Hill, on Charlestown Neck, on the "mainland," there was all manner of confusion. Orders miscarried. Replacements went astray. Requisitions were received that could not be filled. Also, there were some cases of cowardice. The

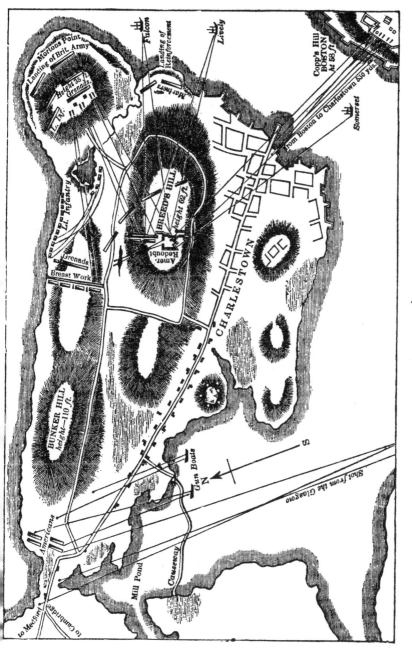

PLAN OF THE BUNKER'S HILL BATTLE

Mortons Point
Landing of Brit. Army
Height 35 ft.
Grenads.
L. INF.
Falcon
Landing of Reinforcement
Mathers
Lively
Copp's Hill
BOSTON
ht 58 ft
Somerset
from Boston to Charlestown 550 Yds
BREED'S HILL
Height 62 ft.
Amer. Redoubt.
CHARLESTOWN
Grenads.
Lt. Infantry
Breast Work
BUNKER HILL
height—110 ft.
Americans
Shot from the Glasgow
S
N
Gun Boats
Mill Pond
Causeway
to Medford
to Cambridge

DR. JOSEPH WARREN

British were peppering the Neck assiduously, and it did not invite, so that some of those who had orders to cross it and to join the beleaguered forces on the peninsula found excuses for failing to do so. When Seth Pomeroy, who was getting on in years, and who had the rank of brigadier general, came to the entrance of the Neck he found it crowded with pausers, the indeterminate. He himself never hesitated. He dismounted, and left his horse, which he said was too valuable a beast to risk in such a place, and crossed the Neck on foot. An even higher ranking officer, Dr. Warren, who only two days before had been created a major general, also crossed on foot. He was suffering from a splitting headache, but he believed that generals should fight, so, having no command (he had not actually received his commission, only notification of it), he went alone. Pomeroy made his way to the rail fence on the left, which looked to him like the spot where the most action might be expected. Dr. Warren went straight to the redoubt, where Colonel Prescott offered to turn over the command to him, an offer the good doctor declined. "I shall be happy to learn from a soldier of your experience," he said. He borrowed a musket and took his place on the firing step.

The New Hampshire men under Reed and Stark likewise crossed the Neck into Charlestown without any casualties, though they kept a steady step, refusing to run. They were late because they had been obliged to make cartridges at the last moment. They paused on the top of Bunker's Hill, a place that appeared to be under the command of Israel Putnam, a Connecticut man, and hence not for them. Stark and Reed, after studying the situation, agreed that the rail fence looked like the stand for them, the place where men were most needed, and they marched down in that direction. (These were the men General Howe had spotted.) John Stark saw that the rail-hay wall did not go clear to the shore of the river—there was a steep embankment there, and room enough for flankers to get around even at high tide—so he set some of his men to work building a stone wall extension, the stones being taken from other walls nearby.

Despite the fact that Lexington-Concord had showed the weaknesses of the new system of fighting with light infantry and grenadier companies mixed, Howe proposed to use this system on his right wing, which he would personally lead, and which was expected to make the breakthrough. A force of almost exactly the same strength—thirty-eight companies to thirty-seven—was the British left wing, in command of Pigot. Pigot did not like the look of Charlestown so near his own extreme left, the end of the line. It was quiet now, but who knew but what it might hold snipers who could harass his men as they started up Breed's Hill? Admiral Graves, who was ashore, asked the peppery little second-in-command if there was anything he could do to help.

"Yes," answered Pigot. "You can burn that village out there for me."

"Certainly," said the admiral, and had himself rowed

back to his flagship, *Somerset,* from which carcasses soon began to arch.

These carcasses, intended to improve upon hot-shot, were black scuttle-like shells filled with oily rags and punched full of holes, and they were fired from ordinary naval guns. Admiral Graves doubtless was glad of a chance to test them against a pretty little community like Charlestown, which consisted of about 400 houses, all wooden.

They were not notably effective. They started a few small smudgy fires, but Graves had to send a detachment of marines ashore with torches before he could get the village really going.

The burning of Charlestown lent a final touch to this martial panorama. When the church steeple crashed, sending upward a shower of sparks, it must have seemed as though the glory of war had received a glad confirmation.

While he was waiting for his reinforcements Howe thought to frighten the enemy with field artillery, and he ordered the brass pieces forward. Because of the soft spots in the earth and the stone walls that had to be opened to admit them, their progress was slow; and when at last they got into a position to fire at the redoubt it was learned that their side boxes contained only 12-pound balls, not 6-pounders as they should have. Howe sent to Boston for 6-pounders and meanwhile he ordered the artillerists to use grape, which they did have; but grapeshot would be effective only at a short distance, and the guns could not be brought that close to the redoubt.

The artillery, on both sides, failed to cover itself with fame.

The reinforcements arrived, the 47th Foot and the 1st Marines, and disembarked at a beach about 200 yards west of Moulton's Point—roughly, halfway between the Point and the blazing village.

At last the order to advance was given.

It was almost half-past three.

# 19

I T WAS the hottest day anyone could remember. In the redoubt and along the breastworks, the digging was finished and the dust had settled, but a burning thirst remained. All they had to drink was rum, and there was not even much of that. Some hogsheads of beer had been sent forth from the supply center at Cambridge, but it disappeared: nobody knew what became of it, but it never got to the boys in the front line.

Howe marched his men slowly. They were carrying more than 100 pounds on their backs, in addition to their guns and cartouche boxes, and he did not want them to arrive on the scene of action already fatigued. Besides, a slow, grim advance might intimidate the rebels. Had there been any artillery opposition he would not have dared to do this, but the few balls the remaining pair of 4-pounders did at last get off sailed over the heads of the soldiers to plop harmlessly into Boston Bay.

Yet the very first company to draw Yankee fire, the light infantry of the Welch Fusiliers, William Howe's own regiment, were trotting at the time. This was on the beach along the Mystick River, at the extreme British right. The infantry-men would be making a frontal assault, true, for they could no longer hope to sneak around the American left flank, there being a defense line where the general, early in the morning, had found only open pasture. Still, it would be a frontal assault against an improvised and obviously shaky fortifica-tion manned by farmers who could be counted upon to shoot too high: even trained regulars tended to aim too high, for the muskets had a terrific shoulder kick, which threw up the muzzle, and it took some time for the ball to get out of that long barrel. The Fusiliers were instructed not to shoot at all but to go in with the bayonet. Those fourteen-inch blades were the terror of Europe, and they would certainly sweep aside the countrymen. The rebels would get in one volley, and conceivably, with luck, they might get in a second, which would be similarly high. Three volleys were unheard of. The bayonets would do the rest; and the bayonets were all on one side.

Behind the breastworks the officers' hardest task was preventing eager inexperienced lads from firing too soon. "Don't shoot till you see the whites of their eyes!" was cried to them.[35] Along the top of the redoubt, on the side facing the advancing redcoats, officers walked, kicking up gun barrels as they went. On the Mystick beach John Stark had planted a stick some thirty-five yards ahead of the stone wall, and he had ordered the men not to shoot until the redcoats passed that stick.

The light infantry of the Royal Welch Fusiliers might have thought as they broke into their dogtrot that they were storming an empty post, that the enemy had already flown, for there was no sound, no sign of movement. There was room for the redcoats seven abreast on the beach, and their muskets were leveled, their bayonets bare.

They passed the stick in the ground.

It was as though they had collided with a cliff. Those who did not fall were stopped in their tracks by the very force of the blast, which seemed to shake the earth under their feet. The oldest officers vowed that they had never seen anything like it. It was not a volley but a continuous *stream* of fire.

Soon above even the sound of that musketry there rose the screams of those writhing on the ground—screams of excruciating pain that were as unnerving to the defenders of the wall as to the companions of the wounded.

It was too much even for the Royal Welch Fusiliers, who broke and ran back down the beach to a place of safety, a place out of range, leaving a vast field of scarlet and white lumps, some twitching, some even crawling, most of them still.

"I never saw so many sheep in a stable," John Stark remarked.

The grenadiers of the King's Own, just to the left, were next. They were advancing against the rail fence, and despite the firing they heard from the beach they could not, because of the embankment, witness the rout of the light infantry. It was not this that flustered them, and certainly not the scrawny obstacle they approached. It was the nature of the pasture beneath their feet. The farmers who owned vegetable gardens and fruit orchards on the Charlestown Peninsula sometimes came over to tend these, but the livestock had long since been driven to the "mainland," lest the British get them, and the grass had grown tall in the pastures. The grenadiers, striving as always to keep perfect order, were forever stumbling over low stone walls or stepping into holes they could not see. At one time they had been overtaken by another grenadier outfit that should have been a prescribed distance behind them, and for a little while there was some highly unmilitary confusion. The King's Own grenadiers had just straightened themselves out after this, and they were peevish as they marched toward an enemy they were hardly thinking of.

The same thing happened to them. It was as though the rail fence had erupted like a volcano. There was a continuous streak of flame, and the grenadiers went down as though cut in swathes by some enormous scythe. They were whirled around. They were knocked right over backward, their feet off the ground.

Other grenadiers came up behind them and made a way

through them—what was left of them—but it was no use. They could not get within bayoneting distance of that inno-cent-looking rail fence. As one of them was to put it: "It was like pushing a wax candle against a red-hot plate—the head of the column simply melted away."

In a matter of minutes the whole British right wing was back at the foot of Moulton's Hill, licking its many wounds. Only *four* of the King's Own grenadiers and only *three* of the light infantrymen of the Welch Fusiliers were alive and unhit.

Though he had been in the thick of it, and was splashed with blood to the thighs, General Howe, every member of whose staff was either dead or wounded, remained un-touched. He was a big man too, a conspicuous target.

Pigot had suffered the same fate on the left wing. His men had never reached the redoubt, but had been driven back from within a few feet of it by a withering fire such as none of them had previously believed possible. Now Pigot was re-forming them, as Howe was re-forming his. They must of course go at it again.

All thought of outflanking the American position was given up. To hell with that river bank, that rail fence! The position could be mopped up later. The only thing to do now—unless they retreated to Boston, which was unthink-able—was join forces for a straight-ahead assault upon the redoubt and breastwork up there. Orders to that effect were given. The men had barely had a chance to catch their breath when they found themselves for the second time climbing that terrible hill.

The Americans were desperately short of gunpowder, but the British did not know this. As far as the British were concerned, the same thing might happen all over again.

And it did. Once again they came reeling down the hill. It was more than human flesh and blood could endure, that terrible fire. It was like trying to march into an open furnace.

This time they were given a somewhat longer breathing

spell, for the confusion was greater and it took much more time to get the men into some kind of order again. This confusion was compounded by a shortage of officers, for the officers had exposed themselves fearlessly in the tradition of the time and had fallen in droves.

General Clinton, watching the fight from Copp's Hill in Boston, saw one group of men milling around on the beach near the still-burning village of Charlestown, and on impulse he ran down to the waterfront and had himself rowed over to that beach and took command of these men, who were otherwise officerless. Some of them were wounded, but they were all willing to have another go at it.

This time the men at least were allowed to dump their packs. As before, they squirmed over stone walls and stepped around the mangled bodies of the fallen, and as before when they were close to the Yankee works they were met with a blast of musketry that caused them to waver, to stop. However, that blast died away. It spluttered out like a turned-down lamp. The last grain of gunpowder in the redoubt and behind the breastwork was gone. You can't fight with rocks and your fists against bayonets. Colonel Prescott ordered a retreat.

It was no rout. There was not a crush at the open back of the redoubt. The men went as swiftly as they could, but they did not turn and run, they did not throw away their muskets.

One of the first to try to climb the redoubt wall—he didn't quite make it—was Major Pitcairn of the Marines. He had been hit several times, and he died in the arms of his oldest son, a lieutenant. He had ten other children at home.

The dust was thick at the back of the redoubt, but it was a blessed dust for the Americans since it caused many redcoats to refrain from shooting lest they kill one of their own kind. The redcoats were coming in from all sides now. They depended largely on cold steel, and they were not gentle with it, for they had been badly shaken.

William Prescott himself got out, one of the last, walking

backward slowly, parrying with his sword the weapons thrust toward him.

This was where the Americans suffered their greatest loss. Once they were out in the open they retreated well, taking whatever cover presented itself, never giving way to panic.

Dr. Warren got out, but not far. His body, a bullet in the head, the jabot and the lovely silver-fringed waistcoat all covered with dust, was found later, behind the redoubt.

The heroes of the rail fence got away in an orderly fashion, and even helped to some extent to cover the retreat of the men from the redoubt.

Driblets of reinforcements were still coming in, and some of these, and notably members of the crack Wethersfield company, having gunpowder, took cover and studiously potted pursuing Britishers.

The last to die was that genial giant Major Andrew McClary, six foot five, of Stark's regiment, a man greatly beloved by those who served under him and who had been a tower of strength in the fighting. He fell on Charlestown Neck itself, and they carried his body away.

On the "mainland" the Americans immediately began to dig in against a possible outflowing from the peninsula, but the British did not push any farther. They'd had enough for one day.

# 20

Not a whit less furious than the events of the battle itself were the charges and counterchanges that flared after the event.

Prescott, still full of fire, wanted to assault the British position and drive them clear out of the peninsula; and fortunately he was overruled. He accused Putnam of hoarding his heterogeneous collection of men at Bunker's Hill instead of leading them into the battle: there must have been more than a thousand militia floundering around on Bunker's Hill—where the entrenchments were not even well begun—instead of helping their fellow countrymen on the firing line.

Charges of cowardice were made against lesser officers, and some of these were tried, a few being convicted and dismissed in disgrace.

The artillery was blamed for the timidity it had displayed, but no formal charges were filed against it, for artillery was hard to come by and should not be offended.

Many of the men in the redoubt and along the breastwork—though not the Connecticut and New Hampshire men who had defended the rail fence—in the course of the battle had developed the rather curious notion that they were being betrayed by their officers, sold out, specifically that sand had been put into the gunpowder to make it less effective. This was not just a wild battlefield rumor. The men, in many cases, really believed it, and continued to believe it after the fighting was finished. The Provincial Congress was obliged to take cognizance of a belief so widely held. The Congress had been deprived of a president in the loss of Joseph Warren, whose death was such a blow to the patriot cause, and they promptly elected as his successor James Warren of Plymouth—no relation. Then the Congress appointed a special committee, consisting of Colonel Cushing, Major Perley, Colonel Prescott, Colonel Barrett, and Deacon Fisher, to investigate the charges of selling out. This committee in time came up with a report exonerating the officers; but the hard feeling remained.

The destruction of that fine old town of Charlestown, too, was thought by many Americans to have been wanton. Not only were some 400 good solid houses and a large number of churches burned to the ground, but many heirlooms, books, and irreplaceable family records that Whigs in Boston had stored in the cellars of friends in Charlestown for fear that in the city they would be seized—these too were lost. It was all very well for Pigot to say that he could not afford to send his men into battle when there might be snipers on his flank, but did he *know*, for *sure*, that there were such snipers? and if so, why hadn't he cleaned them out before he started up the hill? He had the men, he had the time, and the ammunition. The British, indeed, to many Americans had for some time showed themselves too eager to burn Charlestown, perhaps if only to throw the fear of God into the patriots. So this was what they called "civilized" war, as contrasted to the "barbaric" war they encountered in the Yankees?

The British, though they had the hill, had also a staggering casualty list. There was nothing but praise for the personal conduct of William Howe, but there were those, General Clinton prominent among them, who believed and said that Howe should have followed up the break in the battle by pouring out into the "mainland" of Massachusetts and completing the thrashing of the rebel rabble. There were even those, back home in Parliament, who insinuated that the British soldiers had not fought well, a preposterous charge to be leveled against such men, the bravest of the brave.

MAJOR GENERAL WILLIAM HOWE

The British held the peninsula, and they fortified it far more firmly than the Americans had had a chance to do, but they made no move to break out, as the men in the patriot army feared they would. There were several reasons for this. Reinforcements were, again, expected. The men had been badly scared by the battle, and knew now that they were not opposed to mere clowns. Most important, perhaps, the ghastly toll among the officers had made Gage's garrison a tricky one to administer. There was no thought of commissioning sergeants. That just was not done in the British Army. As it stood, the force was out of kilter. It could continue to exist, but it could hardly undertake a major operation. Or at least, so Gage believed.

Howe himself was understandably bitter, though he was silent, about the lack of naval co-operation. Graves' war vessels had pounded away noisily enough, but when, after his rowboat inspection, Howe had asked that a sloop or at least a floating battery be sent up the Mystick River to pepper the rebels from the rear, the request was refused. Admiral Graves was emphatic about this. He did not know the soundings in that river, and neither did he know anything about the currents there. He was making a fine family party out of his job—he had no sons of his own, but three of his four nephews were serving under him on the Boston station, and the fourth was on the way—but though he had been in this place for more than a year, the last two months of it in a state of semi-warfare, he had not taken the trouble to scout a stream less than half a mile from where his flagship was anchored. Had guns been placed in the Mystick, the holding of the rail fence would have been impossible, and Howe's original flanking plan would almost undoubtedly have worked. Yet Howe held his peace.

The small-arms battle, as distinct from the cannonading, had lasted about an hour and a half—from three-thirty to five. The American losses were 115 dead, 305 wounded, 30 missing, most of the last being mortally wounded before their capture. The British lost officially 226 dead, and probably more,[36] and 828 wounded, or at least 45 percent of the force they had put into the field. Nowhere else in modern warfare had there been any such slaughter, in relation to the numbers involved. Nor was there to be again, in this war.[37]

The battle, despite the angry charges that followed it, undoubtedly had elated the Americans and given them confidence in their ability to stand up to the celebrated British regulars, perhaps a little too much confidence.[38] They began to build additional fortifications.

As for the British, they were frankly shocked. The dead privates had been buried in mass graves on the peninsula, the dead officers in churchyards in Boston, and it was in Boston too that the wounded were treated. This was a much more horrifying operation than had been the treatment of the wounded after Lexington-Concord, and as soon as possible the unwanted cripples—what good is a handless man? a man with only one leg?—were being shipped back to England, where the sight of them caused a considerable stir.

*Somebody's* head had to fall. And that somebody, it became clear, would be Thomas Gage, who had served his country faithfully if without any remarkable distinction for more than twenty years in America. Though he was the son of a viscount, he had no title of his own excepting his military title of lieutenant general. The London wits were quick to suggest that he be recalled in order that he might be rewarded by an elevation to the peerage as Lord Lexington, Baron of Bunker's Hill. He was, truly, soon recalled; but there was no forthcoming title. So Gage, too, was a bitter man.

# 21

Just two days before the Battle of Bunker's Hill, a member of the Continental Congress for Maryland, Thomas Johnson, rose in Philadelphia to move "that a general be appointed to command all the continental forces raised or to be raised for the defense of American liberty." John Adams seconded this.

From the beginning it was clear to everyone that the man appointed would have to be a southerner, preferably one from Virginia, easily the most populous and most powerful of the southern colonies. The "wise men of the East," as middle states members and southern members were wont to call the officious New Englanders, until this time had had just about everything their own way; and they were not beloved.

The logical Virginian for the post, the one with the most distinguished military record, such as that was—and who had emphasized his availability by appearing at each session of the Congress, of which he was a member, in his uniform—was Colonel George Washington. So George Washington was appointed that same day, June 15. The delegates were lucky. They could not possibly have found a better man.

Washington accepted the appointment, having declined to consider any manner of wage or prize or honorarium, though he did say that he expected Congress to pay his expenses in the field, of which he promised to make a careful accounting. He bought five new horses, also a light phaeton, and on June 23, a day of dismal rain, he set forth with his staff or "family" and an honor guard of Philadelphia Light Horse.

Three members of the staff were generals just created: Charles Lee, no relation to the Lees of Virginia, who had lately been a lieutenant colonel in the British Army; Horatio Gates, who had held the rank of major in that army; and Philip Schuyler, who was very rich.

Schuyler was to build up and take charge of an Army of the North, with headquarters in Albany. He owned a great deal of the land up in that direction.

Lee was a sarcastic scarecrow highly impressed with his own importance; and Gates was somewhat the same, only less so.

Washington thought that he was weak in making speeches, and though he was an excellent letter writer he did not, at this time, know it. The "family" therefore included two bright young colonels, both Pennsylvania men, Thomas Mifflin, who would write the speeches, and Joseph Reed, who would indite the letters. Reed, a lawyer, was to be especially helpful. However, it was understood that they were both to serve only temporarily, to help get the Commander-in-Chief started. They had their own fortunes to make.

A superb horseman, Washington preferred to ride in that fashion. The phaeton was only for entrances into towns, when, it was hoped, though not perhaps by him, there would be receptions.

When they bedded down for the night in Brunswick, the last stop before New York, they had a problem to ponder. To proceed by way of Staten Island might mean to risk capture, for the British had a warship in the bay and by means of fast launches, if they knew, they could readily pounce upon four whole generals in one fell swoop, a real prize. What was more, Governor Tryon, who had been visiting in England, was to return to New York the very next day, the same day that Washington would enter the town, and Tryon was a convinced, even violent Loyalist. The governor was sure to land at the southern tip of Manhattan Island, the traditional reception spot, and it would be interesting to note which man drew the bigger crowd, for New York, highly important if only because of its strategic location, was reputed to be a Tory stronghold.

It was decided at last to go up the west shore of the Hudson to a wild little place called Hoboken, from where, if everything looked all right, the party could cross to a part of Manhattan that was all country estates.

The plan worked well. Washington, with a plume in his hat, a purple silk sash around his waist, rode through cheering crowds in a carriage drawn by two white horses. The reception he met with was by any standard of comparison superior to that a little later to be accorded to the returning governor. The two never did meet.

It had been Washington's wish to push on as soon as possible, but certain ceremonies had to be acceded to, certain speeches made, and resolutions received. Despite his lack of confidence in this respect, the new Commander-in-Chief presented a fine appearance as orator—tall, handsome, dignified, and obviously in earnest. He had trouble with his teeth (they were wooden) but he enunciated well and clearly. When he assured the assembled dignitaries that "When we assumed the soldier we did not lay aside the citizen," he was wildly acclaimed. Mifflin might have written the line—who knows? —but nobody could have delivered it better than did George Washington.

There had been stray rumors that touched them like ribbons of fog as they left Philadelphia about a battle on the Charlestown Peninsula in Boston Bay; and New York, too, they found, was agog with such rumors, exasperatingly scanty. There was something more. There was in New York an authorized rider for the Massachusetts Provincial Congress who had been passing through with a message addressed to

John Hancock, president of the Continental Congress, a message that was undoubtedly an official report of the battle in question. The rider had been persuaded to linger until the arrival of the Commander-in-Chief, who in turn was persuaded to break the seal and read the message, which was signed by James Warren, the new president of the Massachusetts Provincial Congress. He was reluctant to do this, as he was always to be careful not to offend the Continental Congress; but he at last consented, apologizing in a separate letter later.

It was in this way that he got his first real news of the Battle of Bunker Hill, and it was cheering news, it was challenging. The figures of the British dead and wounded had of course been puffed up, those of the colonial casualties played down; but Washington was no stranger to battle reports, and he could make due allowance.

Next morning, after having dispatched Schuyler in the direction of Albany, he set forth with his party on the Boston Post Road.

They went by the way of King's Bridge; New Rochelle, where the Philadelphia Light Horse after a final salute turned back; New Haven, where Washington, no doubt sighing at this added loss of time, formally reviewed Yale volunteers on the green; Wethersfield; Springfield, Massachusetts; Brookfield. Always there were addresses, bands, cheers, pomp; and always the commander fretted inwardly but retained a serene demeanor.

Sunday, July 2, in the morning, he rode into Watertown, where the Provincial Congress was sitting. They made much of him, but he pushed on that same afternoon, a rainy one, to Cambridge, where, because of sundry false alarms the previous day and that very morning, there was no welcoming committee.

Thus the ride ended, as it had begun, in the rain.

Washington was taken to the house of President Langdon of Harvard, but he did not linger there. He was mounted again and with a glass under his arm in just a few minutes, and he used what was left of the daylight to study the American lines from Roxbury all the way to Prospect Hill.

The next morning, ceremoniously, but with no fanfare, he took command. The sun was shining.

# CHAPTER

# 22

W<small>HAT HE FOUND</small> was a stupendous mess. It was nine days before he could get reports on how many men there were in the camp, and even these reports were probably not correct by the time he received them, since the men were still shifting at will. The "Grand American Army" was supposed to number 16,000 and it might have touched that figure once or twice but it never held it for long. Certainly the army that Washington took over was much smaller than he had been led to expect. It was short of engineers, of blankets, of cannon and gunpowder, of virtually everything else excepting food and blunders.

Once he had put aside the glass and surveyed with a naked eye his more immediate surroundings, the *physical* aspect of that strung-out American camp must have appalled him, for he was a man with a neat mind. He must have winced—though only inwardly—at the ramshackle huts, the varicolored tents, the sloppy sentries, the rags.

The army had at first been overofficered. Now the contrary was true; for "beating orders" had been given out to large numbers of lieutenants and captains, who had thereupon gone forth, usually to their own home towns, to recruit. There were still, however, plenty of generals. Washington had in his wallet commissions for various brigadier general-ships and at least one major generalship, which latter he presented by prearrangement to Old Put Putnam. Most of the others he retained for the present, for he soon learned that there was much bickering about high rank, many of the men who had been major generals in the militia being in the sulks now to find themselves no more than brigadiers with the new Continental Army. All these ruffled feathers were smoothed, but it took time and it took diplomacy and the process vexed Washington, though he himself had always been touchy about his military rank.

One difficulty was that there was no way of telling rank by sight, which meant a waste of time when sentries challenged staff officers who might have swords and even epaulettes but would need a trip back to headquarters to establish their standing. Washington soon arranged for this. He decreed that the Commander-in-Chief himself was to wear a light blue ribbon across his chest between coat and waistcoat, while major generals were to wear purple, brigadiers pink, staff colonels green. He also stipulated that different ranks among the non-staff officers be assigned different colored cockades, so that they might be recognized from a distance or from behind, while N.C.O.'s were to sew a white stripe on top of the left shoulder.

George Washington was not readily shocked in the matter of rough language—and indeed he could uncork a hot flow of profanity of his own whenever his celebrated restraint cracked—but among the commonality and in the course of routine he deemed it bad taste and, worse, bad for discipline; so that one of his first orders, issued the day after he had taken command, July 4, pertained to this: "The General most earnestly requires, and expects, a due observance of those articles of war, established for the Government of the Army, which forbid profane cursing, swearing and drunkenness; And in like manner requires and expects, of all Officers, and Soldiers, not engaged in actual duty, a punctual attendance on divine Service, to implore the blessings of heaven upon the means used for our safety and defence."[39]

Here was a serious matter. And there were to be others; for instance:

"The General does not mean to discourage the practice of bathing whilst the weather is warm enough to continue it, but he expressly forbids, any person doing it, at or near the Bridge in Cambridge, where it has been observed and complained of, that many men, lost to all sense of decency and common modesty, are running about naked upon the Bridge, whilst Passengers, and even ladies of the first fashion in the neighborhood, are passing over it, as if they meant to glory in their shame:—The Guards and Centries at the Bridge, are to put a stop to this practice for the future."[40]

Discipline—actual, enforced, military discipline—had been almost unknown among these New England militiamen when George Washington took command, and it did not please them when he insisted upon it. Yet there were only mutterings, no screams of protest.[41] The new Commander-in-Chief was firm, but not notably harsh. Offenders were drummed out of camp, or they were given extra sentry duties or else told off to dig latrines, and sometimes they might have been made to ride the wooden horse, but there was no running of the gantlet, and the lash at first was limited to Moses' Law—thirty-nine strokes.[42] The men did not seem seriously to resent the lash, the cat-o'-nine-tails. They had been brought up, most of them, in homes where it was firmly believed that to spare the rod was to spoil the child, and they took it for granted that if they did something wrong they would be beaten.

What did shock the General, and to the very depths of his being, was the practice of "leveling"—that is, treating all men, officers or otherwise, as if they were equal. He not only considered this immoral: he believed it to be a very bad military practice.

This was not simple snobbery. He truly believed—he had had it drilled into him since early childhood—that a vast gulf existed between gentlemen and persons who are not gentlemen, and by extension there was such a gulf, seldom if

WASHINGTON SUBDUING A CAMP BRAWL

ever bridgeable, between soldiers with commissions and soldiers without commissions. He thought little enough of the first Massachusetts men he met—"an exceedingly dirty and nasty people" he called them in a letter to his nephew Lund[43] —but he would not let this feeling cloud his military judgment. It was not a social thing with him. He had the liveliest admiration for the up-and-at-'em Israel Putnam, a dirt farmer, an earthy character if ever there was one, and he was later to work well with Brigadier General George Wheedon, who before the war had run a tavern—and not even a very good tavern—in Washington's own colony of Virginia. But the democratic atmosphere at Cambridge jolted him, and he deplored it as inefficient, not to say vulgar.

When he got discouraged, however, he let only a few intimates know it, as when November 28 he wrote to Joseph Reed, who had returned to Philadelphia: "Such a dearth of public spirit, and want of virtue, such stock-jobbing, and fertility in all the low arts to obtain advantages of one kind or another, in this great change of military arrangement, I never saw before, and pray God I may never be witness to again . . . Could I have forseen what I have, and am like to experience, no consideration upon earth would have induced me to accept this command."[44]

You would never have guessed this, to see him.

More material matters troubled him as well. He had been told on his arrival at camp—or as soon thereafter as he could get any answer to his question—that the magazines held 308 barrels of gunpowder, or about 16 tons. This was little enough, and Washington promptly set to work writing to congressmen, governors, and personal friends, begging for more. Then he called a council of war, August 3, and learned that somebody had made a mistake and that there were not 308 barrels left but only 90 barrels.

The first shipment of an order for 1,500 12-foot spears had begun to arrive just before Washington did, but he found them inferior weapons, too short and too brittle, and he ordered more and better ones. True, gunpowder was on its way, thanks in large part to his own efforts, but at the moment they had only those 90 barrels, which would amount to about 9 rounds per man.

If the British had ever sallied forth to attack then it would have been a romp-over. Fortunately the British had troubles of their own.

# CHAPTER

# 23

More than once, in letters to Congress and to friends, the Commander-in-Chief had expressed the wish that the new Continental Army might have a large supply of the so-called hunting shirts, a longish skirted garment of butternut brown, with a frilled cape over the shoulders, worn with leggins and moccasins—it was in fact originally an Indian outfit—and with a round coonskin cap, the tail hanging behind. Such a dress, almost a uniform along the frontier, as Washington knew from his experiences there, was unknown in the vicinity of Cambridge or indeed anywhere in New England excepting perhaps in the wilder portions of the New Hampshire Grants (Vermont). Washington knew how practical it was, cheap, convenient, as comfortable in cold weather as in hot, and with its neutral hue not easily spotted in either woods or fields. It was made, ordinarily, of Ticklenburgh, or tow cloth.

He was soon to see too much of this garb.

As a part of its effort to bring into the conflict men from other colonies besides those of New England, the Continental Congress recently had authorized the raising of six companies of riflemen in western Pennsylvania, two in Maryland, and two in Virginia, a total of 1,430 men. The lists were over-subscribed. The rude frontiersmen thought that war would be a fine idea, for they yearned to shoot something besides bears and Indians. They elected their own officers, but these meant even less to them than did their officers to the rank and file of the various New England militias.

They came swinging into camp July 25, and then again

August 5 and August 7, having marched anywhere from 500 to 700 miles without a single case of sickness. Tall, broad-shouldered, rugged men, many of them with beards, they all carried their beloved rifles.

The rifle was almost as great a rarity in those parts as the hunting shirt, with which it was irrevocably linked. The *principle* was by no means new.[45] For many years men had known that by cutting spiraled grooves into the inside of a gun barrel they could cause a bullet fired through that barrel to spin in the air. Such a bullet would not wobble like a musket bullet, and thus was much more accurate. It would travel faster and therefore farther than a musket bullet: it could kill at 200 yards or even more.

The firing mechanism, the lock, was the same as that of a musket. Barrel and butt might be much the same too, except for the rifling inside the barrel. But because of that very rifling the frontier gun took longer to reload. With the rifled fowling pieces some sportsmen used it was necessary to hammer the powder and ball down into the barrel with a mallet. A musket ball often fit in there in a loose manner, held in place by the wadding. The rifle ball had to be snug in place or the rifling would have no effect upon it as it passed through the barrel. *Being* snug, it wasted none of the expanding gases from the explosion, and this was one of the reasons why it could be counted upon to carry much farther than would a musket ball.

The military objection to the rifle was, it would seem, a damning one—the slowness of reloading. The frontiersmen who developed the so-called Kentucky rifle (which actually came from Pennsylvania) had improved the reloading speed by the invention of round linen patches, each about the size of a half-dollar. The ball was wrapped in one of these patches, and the whole thing was dipped into bear grease before being rammed down the rifle barrel. Even so, a good musketeer could get off three shots while a rifleman was getting off one, and still have a bayonet with which to protect himself against a charging foe: the rifle did not take a bayonet.

The rifleman did carry his powder in a horn, and he carried his precut balls in a small leather sack hung at his waist with that horn. His weapon was economical of powder and ball as compared with the musket, for he could make every shot count. This was important to a man who might have to spend weeks on end in the forest without access to any manner of magazine. Few of the westerners who swarmed into Cambridge camp had ever even heard of a cartridge.

A rifled gun fouled much more readily than a smoothbore, and had to be cleaned more often.

Because of the great distances they had covered in such startlingly short times the "shirtmen," as they soon came to be called, were excused from routine camp duties—at first. They took advantage of this. With time on their hands, they would slip forth in pairs or alone to stalk British sentries as they might have stalked deer at home. The sentries, finding themselves winged at distances that just the other day would have been thought impossible, soon grew wary; but the riflemen went right on taking potshots at them. This was wasteful of powder.

When a man with a musket finished his sentry duty he was expected to unload his weapon, for leaving those things around loaded was an edgy business. Also, there were times when he had reason to believe that his powder had got damp, though he could not be sure. He preferred on the latter occasion to take the gun outside of camp and point it into the air and pull the tricker. If it went off, then he knew that the powder had been dry. If not—and this is what he was *supposed* to do always—he would use a long ramrod-like instrument called a worm in order to draw the charge: the worm had a sort of corkscrew at its lower end.

Shooting guns in order to learn whether the powder was dry was strictly forbidden in the Continental camp, but that made little difference to the riflemen from Pennsylvania, Maryland, and Virginia. They had their own way of doing things, and if they did not have to pay for the powder why bother to save it? The charge in a rifle could be removed with the same worm that the musketeer used, but the process was much more tedious. The rifleman usually just went to the edge of the encampment and let fly into the air, thereby quite possibly—it had happened more than once—creating an alarm and bringing men at a trot, for that they thought the camp was being attacked.

When an attempt was made to set these proud personages to work on everyday chores there was trouble. When one of their number for a petty infringement of camp rules was arrested and put into prison, there was more trouble. The riflemen tore the jail apart and released him.

Soon there was a full-fledged riot. It took place near Prospect Hill (sometimes called Mount Pisgah) September 10, and George Washington himself was largely instrumental in breaking it up, for he charged in on foot and showed no gentleness. They were rough, those riflemen, but no rougher than the tall Virginian with the huge hands, the brawny shoulders, the quiet voice.

Thirty-three riflemen were arrested as a result of that riot, and it was hard to know what to do with them. The *un*arrested ones certainly would not sit by and see their comrades thrown into jail, much less lashed, a punishment with which they were not familiar. At last the thirty-three were fined twenty shillings each.

When Benedict Arnold visited Cambridge to enlist men for his proposed expedition to Montreal and Quebec, a large number of these riflemen joined up, for they had found life in camp dull, and perhaps they longed for the wilderness again: Arnold proposed to go overland, through Maine. This considerably relieved the situation at Cambridge.

Before Quebec—which city failed to fall—one of these

strapping fellows was captured alive, complete with coonskin cap, hunting shirt, and 7-foot firearm. He was sent to England, where he created a short-lived sensation, much as had, earlier, the first red Indian brought back by John Smith, the first Eskimo brought back by Martin Frobisher.

As far as the Commander-in-Chief was concerned, they could have sent them *all* to England.

# 24

Tʜᴇ ɴᴇᴡ Continental Army was the best paid army in the world, when it *was* paid. A private got the equivalent of $6⅔ a month, a lieutenant $13⅔, a captain $20, a brigadier $125, a major general $166. These were sensational wages, and though they might sometimes be late in arriving they were at the time of the siege of Boston always in hard cash, for the vicious paper currency had not yet been devised and property seized from Loyalists was still sufficient to pay the troops.

Some undecorated hero in the American camp took advantage of this, as well as of the notoriously unappetizing food served in Boston, when he caused to be printed on small sheets of paper, suitable for going with the wind, this interesting comparison:

| PROSPECT HILL | BUNKER'S HILL |
|---|---|
| (the principal fortification facing Charlestown Neck) | |
| I. Seven dollars a month. | I. Three pence a day. |
| II. Fresh provisions and in plenty. | II. Rotten salt pork. |
| III. Health. | III. The scurvy. |
| IV. Freedom, ease, affluence, and a good farm. | IV. Slavery, beggary, and want.[46] |

These were released whenever the breeze was right. What effect they may have had is not a matter of record, but certainly they infuriated the British officers, who forbade the men even to pick them up on penalty of all manner of brutal punishment, which suggests that the fear of desertion, a fear that always hung like a dark cloud above any British Army camp of the time, at least had not diminished.

The two sides scowled fiercely, like a couple of small boys circling each other, each uttering dire threats but unprepared to do more than that: "one was afraid and the other dassent."

Early in the siege there had been a certain try at correspondence between General Lee on the American side and General Burgoyne on the British, old army friends; but this, on the advice of the Continental Congress, which feared that it might seem to smack of treason to the men, soon was dropped. However, when Washington and Gage, the two top men, began to exchange letters about prisoners, everything was smooth, if painfully proper. They too had been friends years ago in the British Army, both having served under Braddock.

Washington had heard that the Americans the British held were all lodged together, men and officers alike, and this raised his ire, so that his opening letter to Gage was a stiff one and sizzled with indignation.

Gage, no doubt with Gentlemen Johnny Burgoyne hanging over his shoulder, replied:

"Britons, ever preëminent in mercy, have outgone common examples, and overlooked the criminal in the captive. Upon these principles, your prisoners, whose lives, by the laws of the land, are destined to the cord, have hitherto been treated with care and kindness, and more comfortably lodged than the king's troops in the hospitals; indiscriminately, it is true, for I acknowledge no rank that is not derived from the king."

Washington came back with:

"You affect, sir, to despise all rank not derived from the same source with your own. I cannot conceive one more honorable than that which flows from the uncorrupted choice of a brave and free people,—the purest source and original fountain of all power. Far from making it a plea for cruelty, a mind of true magnanimity and enlarged ideas would comprehend and respect it."

Gage made no reply to this, and Washington, as he had threatened to do, commanded that the handful of British officers he held be taken from Watertown and Cape Ann and confined to the common jail at Northampton with the enlisted men. However, he did not keep this up. In a few days he relented and ordered the officers released again on parole. After all, they *were* officers.

The British did a great deal of drilling, right out on the Boston Common and especially on the Charlestown Common, which could readily be seen from the American lines, and they also held many boat drills with small craft from the war vessels. These may have been meant only to keep the men busy, to discourage them from devising, or perceiving, ways in which to desert; or they could have been intended to frighten the rebels. If the latter was the case, they could be said to succeed. The Continentals had a long line to watch, from Chelsea clear around to Dorchester Neck, and the fortifications the British had erected on the peninsula of Charlestown looked ominous, as did those boat drills. The Continentals strengthened their own fortifications at Roxbury and at Cambridge, and they built breastworks and placed cannon at Prospect Hill, Winter Hill, and Plowed Hill, for the avowed purpose of halting a possible breakout over Charlestown Neck.

The British would start a bombardment of Plowed Hill or Roxbury or wherever, every time, it would seem, that they happened to think of it, perhaps for the purpose of proving how much gunpowder and how many balls they had. The Americans would answer only intermittently and briefly, just to show that they *could*. Neither side did any damage, except that in the American camp the practice of chasing the balls for souvenirs as they rolled along the ground caused some serious burns and in two cases death. An order went out from Washington's headquarters—he had moved to the house of John Vassal, a Loyalist who had fled to Boston[47]—forbidding this risky practice; but the practice was continued.

It had been an exceptionally warm summer, but even salted food must be cooked, and long before the leaves began to turn the supply of firewood in Boston was running low. Rail fences disappeared overnight, and trees were surreptitiously chopped down. Prices went up, and especially the price of cordwood, when you could get any at all. The British had converted the Old South Church into a riding academy but even they would hardly dare to tear down the houses of Boston one by one. Yet—how else were they to keep warm when winter came?

The smallpox epidemic had not abated, but rather increased, and now that fresh food was in such short supply scurvy, understandably, was prevalent. It was a debilitating disease that made the eyes sunken, the gums spongy and bloody, the muscles all one ache. Men did not often die of scurvy, but they suffered horribly—and they stank. It was a most unpleasant malady to nurse.

Of course the fresh food, when there was any, went to the sick, who increased alarmingly nonetheless. The harbor islands, in a series of skirmishes, had been cleaned out of livestock and fodder alike, and in their desperation the British ranged farther afield, pouncing upon places where they were least expected, such as Connecticut in the neighborhood of New London, and the islands of Long Island Sound, from which they returned on one memorable occasion with more than 100 head of oxen and about 1,800 sheep. An anonymous wit in the *London Chronicle* caused all the capital to laugh with his comments on this bit of plundering:

> "In days of yore the British troops
>   Have taken warlike kings in battle;

But now, alas! their valor droops,
  For Gage takes naught but—harmless cattle.

Britons, with grief your bosoms strike!
  Your faded laurels loudly weep!
Behold your heroes, Quixote-like,
  Driving a timid flock of—sheep."

Tempers were short in Boston, nerves were frayed, and the men would have liked nothing better than an order to march forth to battle. Such an order never came. Gage, a broken man, sailed for home October 10, but Howe, who succeeded to the command, was not a whit more enterprising, so that things bumbled along in the same old groove.

# 25

Benjamin Church, Jr., was a physician with a good practice, but he was keeping a woman and that costs money, so he took up another profession on the side—he became a spy.

He must have been a great find, for he had been noisy in the patriots' cause. He was a friend of both Warrens, of John Hancock, Samuel Adams, James Otis. He was a member of the powerful Committee of Safety, which ruled Massachusetts, and until the coming of Washington virtually ruled the army in the field. He had been chosen to deliver the chief oration on the anniversary of the Boston Massacre, a very great honor. He was not a member of the Continental Congress, but as a member of the Massachusetts Provincial Congress he had been sent to wait upon the Continental body in Philadelphia and to carry to it a plea for a united army and one commander. A graduate of Harvard and of the London Medical College, he was Washington's surgeon-general and director of hospitals. He was a poet of some standing, forty-four years old, and lived in an elegant house just outside Boston. In other words, he was the last person anyone would suspect of being a spy.

He did not sell out suddenly, on impulse, afterward bitterly to repent. He had been carrying on correspondence with General Gage for some time, and had been paid regularly.

The cause of his downfall was another of those almost unbelievably stupid moves so often associated with the world of undercover agents.

As a physician he was a privileged person who sometimes traveled inside of the British lines and back again, so that he could pass on his information orally. As the siege tightened, however, this became increasingly inconvenient, and he had to depend upon the written word. He would write seemingly personal letters to his brother-in-law in Boston, John Fleming, a printer and a Loyalist; but these letters were undoubtedly meant for General Gage. In the middle of September this husband of his sister began to worry about the good doctor, who was becoming more prominent every day in the patriot cause. With Hancock and both of the Adamses away in Philadelphia as delegates to the Continental Congress, Dr. Church was one of the brightest of the leading lights in Massachusetts independence circles, and this alarmed the Boston printer, who seemingly was not aware of his brother-in-law's secret connections, and who wrote urging that Church close his affairs, cut off from his associates, and flee into Boston to make his peace with the King's forces, which, Fleming was sure, would soon prevail. Church took alarm. He wrote an answer that was a farrago of inflated figures about the strength of the Continental Army. He seemed, almost hysterically, to be trying to convince his brother-in-law that the rebels were much stronger than he, Fleming, supposed. However, his regular channel for the transmission of such letters through the lines was temporarily closed, and since his inamorata was about to visit relatives in Newport, Rhode Island, he entrusted the epistle to her, instructing her to see that it got into the hands of a certain British naval officer, one Captain Wallace, who would take it to Boston.

The lady in question doubtless had many talents, but she was not very bright. In Newport she went to a friend, Godfrey Wainwood, a man with whom she had previously had an affair; but when he, for reasons of his own, refused to take her to see Captain Wallace, she left the letter with him and returned to Cambridge.

Wainwood, who was a baker, was worried. His own loyalty was to the rebel cause, and after fretting for a few days, and after consulting a like-minded friend, he opened the letter.

What he saw was not rewarding. It was gibberish, not even English, a multitude of tiny squiggly figures that would seem to represent letters of the alphabet. Wainwood, not knowing what to do, presently did nothing; but when a little later he got a note from the woman in Cambridge asking him why the letter had not been forwarded, he was really worried. How did *she* know that the letter had not been received in Boston? Wainwood went to the camp at Cambridge and put the matter before the chief of the Rhode Island militia, Nathanael Greene, one of the new brigadier generals. Greene had one look at the thing and took it and Wainwood both to Washington, asking for a private audience.

The message made no sense to Washington, but he inquired and learned that there were two amateur cryptographers in the camp, one a chaplain, the Reverend Mr. West, the other a Massachusetts militia colonel, Elisha Porter. The letter was submitted to these two men separately, and in a very short time they came up with identical decipherings. It has been absurdly easy, child's play, the simplest kind of substitutional. All they'd had to do was use their frequency tables.[48]

Even then the message did not make sense, since its figures were exaggerated, and it read more like a wild plea for the patriot cause than a betrayal of military secrets. Nevertheless, it still *smelled* wrong. It was fetid, as it lay there on the table, the men staring down at it.

Washington had the woman picked up for questioning. She held out for four hours, and then she broke and gave them the name of Dr. Church, a stunner.

Dr. Church, confronted with the letter, readily admitted that he had written it. He refused to say why he had used a cipher, but he did contend that since the letter was addressed to his brother-in-law, a civilian, it was not treasonous. He had only been trying to promote peace, he said. They locked him up.

His house was searched and his papers confiscated, but there was evidence that somebody had been there earlier and that many of the papers were missing, recently removed. No proof of wrongdoing was found.

There was a council of war October 3 and 4, and it found Dr. Church guilty; but it could not set a punishment for the embarrassing reason that the articles of war under which it operated did not specify any punishment for such a crime. Bewildered, the council turned over Dr. Church to his fellow members of the Provincial Congress, who tried him, October 27, in the church at Watertown, their meeting place. He defended himself at great length, if not with great clarity, from an improvised prisoner's dock in the church aisle;[49] but the delegates were not convinced, and they declared him to be "utterly expelled," and decreed that he should be locked up in a remote place and not allowed visitors or writing materials. He was taken to the town jail at Norwich, Connecticut,[50] and Washington, a badly shaken Commander-in-Chief, went back to his work of building an army.

# CHAPTER

# 26

THE WAR was proving vexatious in its refusal to flicker out. Neither side had expected it to drag along like this; for the redcoats had believed that patriotic ardor would wane and the farmers would soon return to their manure piles, whereas the former minutemen affirmed that as soon as the ministers in London realized that they, the former minutemen, meant business, then there would be held out, if tremulously, an olive branch. But nothing of the sort happened. Nor was there any activity along military lines, only an occasional amphibious encounter, a snappy little dogfight scarcely worth labeling a skirmish.

Washington himself was as impatient as any, more so than most. Always a thin-skinned man, he had come to fear that the rest of the country was calling him a coward, or at least thinking of him that way. Why didn't he do something? Why did he just sit there, using hard-raised money? Few of them had any notion of the mass of administrative details that he had to face every day. But—generals were supposed to fight and win battles, weren't they? Then why didn't he *do* something?

September 11, the day after the Prospect Hill riot, two weeks before the arrest of Benjamin Church, Washington at a council of war proposed an attack on Boston by means of rowboats. It sounded mad; or at least it sounded so to the rest of the council, who were unanimously against it, so that the subject was dropped.

The British were masters of the sea and of Boston Bay and the small waters surrounding the bay, but hidden in a hundred places were rowboats, most of them whaleboats, which it was proposed to use, exploiting the element of surprise. Boston Neck, of course, would be assaulted at the same time, but only as a feint.

October 18 Washington proposed the same plan, and again the council determinedly voted it down.

November 2 the council took under consideration a plan to seize and hold the whole of the Dorchester Peninsula, but nothing was done.

It was getting cold.

As he came to know the men better, Washington was relying more and more on his council of war, which as a rule was limited to major generals and brigadiers. Also, he continued to be scrupulously open in his dealings with the Continental Congress, informing them of everything, introducing nothing of significance without having first consulted with them at long distance. Congress responded by granting most of his requests. When he asked for a paymaster general he got one, as when he asked for a provost marshal and judge advocate. At last a Congressional "committee of conference" called in person at Cambridge to see if there was not something more that they could do.

This committee consisted of Benjamin Franklin, just back from England, Thomas Lynch, a wealthy South Carolina planter, and Benjamin Harrison of Virginia, a broad man who liked broad jokes. It arrived in camp October 15, called upon George Washington, and afterward, from the 18th to the 22nd, conferred with various New England state officials. At all times the understanding was that the army was to be controlled by the civilians.

What it was proposed to do, by Washington, was to withdraw one army and install another in its place, bringing about for the first time uniformity of company and regiment sizes and the appointment rather than the election of field officers, and all this without gunpowder and within a few hundred feet of the enemy's outposts. The first of the year would tell the tale, for it was then that most of the militia enlistments ran out.

The men in camp, still changing all the time, coming and going, were not yet ready to face the enemy in a stand-up fight. They would need more training for that—and more muskets, of which there was now a serious shortage, and more gunpowder.

The American fortifications were, admittedly, strong; and when on October 10 General Gage sailed away and General Howe took over the command, Howe, remembering Breed's Hill, was in no hurry to mount an attack. Howe would have liked to meet the Americans in an open field, but this, for the present, was impossible. He could only wait. He was a good waiter.

There were a few high moments. A Continental privateer named Manly, commissioned by Washington himself—though the British called him a pirate and probably would have hanged him as such if they had caught him—in November just outside of Boston Bay nabbed a big supply brig named *Nancy*, and that was a prize indeed: no powder, but 100,000 flints, 2,000 muskets complete with bayonets, and a great brass mortar of 13-inch caliber, a weapon that weighed more than 2,700 pounds. Old Put Putnam christened this gun "the Congress" that very night, using a bottle of rum; and many men came to see it; but it could not be fired without powder.

They had a white Christmas that year, but though the camp was using 117 cords of firewood a day, the cold was not intense enough to freeze solid the Mystick, Back Bay, and the mouth of the Charles. Washington had been hopeful for such a freezing, for he had plans to take either Boston or Charlestown or both by crossing the ice at many different points and hitting the fortified areas from behind. Nothing ever came of these plans.

January 1 was a cold wet day, with the wind harsh from the northwest. A few days after that, the British saw to it that many copies of the speech from the throne, which had been delivered October 26, reached the rebel camp. If the British had expected this to cause consternation they were disappointed. The speech was almost unbelievably violent, killing any hope of honorable reconciliation. It had been the custom among the colonists until this time to lay all the blame for what they viewed as outrageous tyranny on Parliament or, even more, upon the ministers of the cabinet, rather than on the King, who still was popularly pictured as a kindly man misled by rascals. The enemy, even in official reports, frequently were referred to as the "ministerial forces," or the "ministerialists." The October 26 speech from the throne did more than anything else to change this attitude, painting George III as he really was, a pigheaded fool.

Gentleman Johnny Burgoyne, he of the political connections, had sailed back to England for the purpose of trying to wangle himself an independent command in Canada, but he had left behind him a hilarious farce called *The Siege of Boston*, which had a clown as Washington and many other amusing features. This was staged, in Gentleman Johnny's absence, in Faneuil Hall the night of January 8, and it was a howling success—for as long as it lasted. It was interrupted by a sergeant who dashed into the hall shouting that the rebels were attacking Charlestown. Since the whole show, thus far, had been the wildest kind of slapstick, it was assumed that this announcement was simply another comedy interlude, and the officers who composed the audience greeted it with roars of laughter. When the laughter had abated, however, musketry could be heard—from the direction of Charlestown. The officers ran to turn out their men—some of them, from the stage itself, in women's clothes, some in blackface.

Blackface or whiteface, skirts or uniforms, they were too late. Thomas Knowlton of rail fence fame with 200 picked men had paid the Charlestown Peninsula a jarring visit, encircling the redoubt to leap upon the town, where they killed one redcoat, took five prisoners, and burned eight of the remaining fourteen houses, without suffering a scratch.

The second half of Burgoyne's play was not as funny as the first.

A council of war a little earlier had estimated the British strength in Boston at 11,500 (which was too much, but not *much* too much) and had decided that the Continental Army should have just twice that, or 23,000, in order to be sure of holding the British in. The Cambridge camp in fact never even approached this figure, and as 1775 faded and 1776 came on it was at one of its lowest points. On paper, the crisis had passed. The old mixed-up mass of militia units was gone, more or less, and a new united Continental Army stood in its place, a masterpiece of reorganization. In practice, this was not so. The promised enlistees did not appear. The militamen who had agreed to do so did not enlist in the regular army. Washington, who had offered three months'advance pay to any and all recruits, now was obliged to admit that he no longer had enough for more than one month of advance pay; whereupon a great deal of enthusiasm evaporated.

Much had been expected of the double-pronged attack upon Canada, an attack led by the British Army veteran Richard Montgomery, a tall, thin, mild-mannered, balding gentleman, and his second-in-command, the redoubtable, the unpredictable Benedict Arnold; but though Montreal had been taken—and still was being held by a handful of Continentals under General Wooster—Quebec, a much more important city, had refused to fall. Now Montgomery was dead, and Arnold lay with a smashed leg on a hospital cot while his men deserted in droves. It was true that Benedict Arnold still vowed his intention of conquering Canada if he had to do it *alone,* and true too that those who knew him best said that he was quite capable of trying that; but from Cambridge it looked as though the northern campaign had fizzled out.

Worse, it was patent to the dullest observer that the British were preparing a big expedition in Boston. Transports were being readied, powder and ball and food rations were being loaded aboard them. This would not be any petty cattle raid but a first-class military operation. Against what? Against New York? It looked so. And New York, all unprotected, together with Westchester County to the north and Long Island to the east, notoriously was a hotbed of Toryism. Once the British had taken New York—and it should be like knocking an overripe apple out of a tree—they could fortify the line of the Hudson River, dividing the colonies into two parts and leaving Washington and the main army with redcoats behind and redcoats ahead, a pretty pickle.

Washington was sick with anxiety inside as he went about his duties with a calm manner, an imperturbable face.

One ray of hope remained. That brash young man named Henry Knox—if he somehow got through everything might yet be saved.

CHAPTER

# 27

Henry Knox was missing two fingers of his left hand, the result of a gun accident on a duck-shooting picnic; but he was not missing much else.

He was ebullient. He bounced. He had just turned twenty-five, yet he must have weighed ten times that many pounds. He carried this bulk gracefully, however, for he was six feet tall and had a military bearing; also, he was dapper in his dress. He had merry blue-gray eyes, a somewhat prematurely bulbous nose, a high complexion.

He had been born July 25, 1750, the son of a poor Scotch-Irish shipmaster who died early. Henry, one of many children, had had very little schooling, but he had taught himself vigorously and well, being proficient even in the use of French, though he had never traveled. His specialty was military science: he could never get enough books on that subject. He was a lieutenant in and second-in-command of the Boston Grenadiers, a swank militia outfit.

As a boy he had worked in a bookshop, and at twenty-one he set up an establishment of his own. It was called the New London Book Shop, located in William's Court, and it was one of eight in Boston at the time. Like virtually all American merchants, he was in debt all the time: it was a part of the system, and one of the reasons for the Revolution.

He had plenty of customers, but he had plenty of time too, and he read and read and read. His shop became something of a conversational headquarters for the young intellectuals. It also became a point of suspicion on the part of the occupation officers, for Paul Revere was often seen there, and James Warren, and John Adams.

One of Henry Knox's most frequent customers was Lucy Flucker, who was eighteen years old, pretty, full in the figure, and daughter of the Secretary of the Colony of Massachusetts, Thomas Flucker. The Fluckers were a high-toned family, and, naturally, Tory. Young Knox's Whiggish views were well known—he did not shout them from the rooftops but neither did he try to hide them—and Thomas Flucker forbade the match, for all the good *that* did him. They were married in July of 1774, and a very successful union it turned out to be.

The Fluckers tried to buy Knox over to the Loyalist side with the offer of a commission in the British Army—for nothing. It must have strongly tempted the young bookseller, not only as a piece of property but even more as a grand experience; but he refused, giving no reason for his refusal.

When feeling mounted higher, and it became certain that a clash was near, the young couple made arrangements to clear out of Boston. Knox's store and its stock were sure to be confiscated anyway; and the redcoats could confiscate his accumulated bills too, if they wished.

Soon after the day of Lexington and Concord they made it, a highly romantic dash. He had to leave his self-bought grenadier's uniform behind, which was a wrench because it was polychromatic to a degree, but he could not bear to part with his sword, which Lucy hid under her skirts when they passed through the lines. They settled, more or less, in Worcester.

Knox did not ask for a post in the Continental artillery, which he would dearly have loved; but he let the post ask for him. Meanwhile he busied himself as a civilian consultant, for he was widely read in matters of military engineering, and had his own ideas about how a redoubt should be built. He was very useful. There were those who thought that Lucy was putting on airs, but everybody liked Lucy's husband.

Washington met this effervescent young man soon after his arrival in Cambridge to take over—and make over—the Continental Army. He was immediately impressed. Knox might talk big, but he could act big as well. He was by no means all wind. He got things done.

Here was the beginning of a beautiful professional friendship. These two men appreciated each other from the start; and through all the dark years that were to follow they worked smoothly together for the glorification of America.

Washington was with Charles Lee at the time of the meeting, and they asked the burly young civilian to show them over the fortifications at Roxbury, which he, Knox, had helped to design and to construct. He assented readily, and they listened with care. Washington often asked for Knox's advice after that. The subject of the guns at Fort Ticonderoga came up many times, and Knox was keen to get the job. He was a city boy, who knew nothing about sleds and sledges and sleighs and ice runners, nothing about the hiring of oxen and horses or how to get the most out of such beasts. But he was sure that he could bring those guns all the way from Ticonderoga to Cambridge, once some snow had fallen and the rivers had frozen solid. He just *knew* that he could.

His confidence was contagious. Washington became convinced that here was, indeed, the man.

The almost weaponless artillery arm was headed by Colonel Richard Gridley, who was middle-aged and ailing, and who, it was agreed, no longer would serve in the field. There were two lieutenant colonels, and it was rather well understood that one of these would be created a full colonel, though at the same time it was equally well understood that the loser would probably resign in a rage. Knox, a younger man than either of the aspirants, was offered, through John Adams as a member of the Continental Congress, one of the lieutenant colonelcies. He refused.

He was outspoken about it. He wanted the full colonelcy or nothing. "I have the most sacred regard for the liberty of my country and am fully determined to act as far as in my power in opposition to the present tyranny attempted to be imposed upon it—but as an honor is comparative I humbly hope that I have as good pretensions to the rank of Col as many now in the service . . . If your respectable body should not incline to give the rank and pay of Col. I must beg to decline it. But I will do every service in power as a Volunteer."

Even so, Washington thought that Knox should go after those guns, to which Knox readily complied. Washington wanted above all a good clear statement of how many guns and how many barrels of powder and how many trained or partly trained artillerists the Continental Army had or could be expected to have soon. Knox, as a civilian, first made a survey of the artillery in or near the Cambridge camp, and reported on *that,* a sad lot. Then Washington gave him a letter to the Continental commander at New York and at the same time wrote to General Schuyler in Albany to tell him that he might expect Knox soon and to beg him to help the young fellow in every possible way to bring those guns down from Ticonderoga.

". . . no trouble or expense must be spared to get" the guns, Washington had written in his order.

In the middle of November, then, Henry Knox and his younger brother, William,[51] together with one servant, bade a tearful farewell to Lucy in Worcester and set forth on horseback for New York. It was the first visit any of them had ever paid to that city, which tremendously impressed them with its grand homes, its miles of waterfront, its bustle, its genteel if undeniably Toryish inhabitants, though Henry did complain, in his diary, that everything in New York *cost* so much.

It took him only two days to get his artillery survey made, and by that time he was a full colonel in the Continental Army, though he did not yet officially know it.

By some miracle—or conceivably some invisible political pressure, for John Adams favored young Knox, and Adams was a powerful man to have on your side—the two contending lieutenant colonels of the Continental artillery agreed to remain in that rank, each speaking in favor of Henry Knox as the full colonel, a commission Washington was prompt to issue.

November 28 they set forth for Ticonderoga.

# CHAPTER

## 28

THEY WERE ON HORSEBACK, and they made good time, averaging forty miles a day.

December 1 they reached Albany, where Philip Schuyler, if a trifle condescending, was helpful. They stayed there two days.

Albany thrilled a somewhat naïve Knox, who reported in a letter to Lucy that "from its situation, and commanding the trade of the water and the immense territories westward, must one day be, if not the capital, yet nearly it, of America."

December 3 they easily did the thirty-five miles to Saratoga, where they made some further arrangements about transport. The next day they rode thirty miles to Fort George[52] at the southern tip of Lake George, a body of water that extended in a generally northern way more than thirty miles to Fort Ticonderoga and the southern tip of Lake Champlain. They spent the night at Fort George, where the colonel got off two hasty messages before plunging into the wilderness, one to General Washington, one to Lucy: "I took this opportunity to write to the dearest object of my affections, beleive [*sic*] me I think continually of you." That morning (of the 5th), leaving their horses, they went by boat to Ticonderoga[53]—and the prize.

The haul was indeed immense. Dozens, scores of huge black cannon awaited the inspection of the eager chief of artillery, who found many of them in reasonably good condition. He soon set about cataloguing them as to weight, caliber, capacity, and type of metal, and he selected fifty-nine to go south with him.[54]

These included forty-three cannon, thirty of them iron, thirteen brass, ranging from 4-pounders to 24-pounders, besides mortars, howitzers, and cohorns, also a barrel of flints and twenty-three boxes of lead. Washington had particularly cautioned Henry Knox to include the barrel of flints—an estimated 30,000 of them—for the flints from that part of the country were considered the best in the world for musket locks as well as for arrowheads.

Some of the pieces were as short as one foot in the barrel, some as long as eleven. There were guns that weighed only 100 pounds and there were three 13-inch mortars that weighed more than a ton each. The total was estimated at 119,000 pounds, or almost sixty tons.

All this was to be hauled more than 300 miles in the middle of winter.

Most of the pieces were mounted, and the job of getting them off their carriages was an arduous one. Knox wrote out a set of instructions for the road movement. The heavier pieces were to go first, the lighter ones later. All should be loaded with the vents and touchholes down. One pair of oxen would be expected to haul at least 1,000 pounds.

There were three types of boats in use on the lakes—gondolas, which were nothing at all like the Venetian vehicles but were in reality scows; bateaux, or double-ended flat-bottomed boats; and piraguas, which were smaller and lighter. All were masted and could be sailed if there was a fit wind, or rowed if there was a calm or a contrary wind.

It was in these boats, manned in part by soldiers from Ticonderoga, in part by civilian employees from the neighborhood of Fort George, that they started south, Saturday, December 9. The chief of artillery went ahead in a piragua, in order to make things ready at Fort George. He and his companions spent a few hours that night at Sabbath Day Point, where a party of Indians bedded down with their squaws in a hut gave them roast venison. The next day, Sunday, the wind veered, making the sail useless. Even with all hands straining at the oars they could barely make headway, and it took them all day to cover the last ten miles.

Lake George is only three miles wide at its widest point. The water along the banks was frozen, but not solidly, being masses of grinding ice chunks; while the middle was clear. When his younger brother did not appear with the greater part of the fleet, Henry Knox, in a few days, sent a fast boat to inquire. William, it appeared, had let one of the scows go aground on a sunken rock near Sabbath Day Point. It had not gone far under, however, and after a night of backbreaking work the men salvaged it, mortars and all, and repaired it, and got it afloat. This had used up all of one day, and the men were so exhausted afterward that they had to be allowed a full night's sleep. Everything was all right now.

It took them almost a week to make the thirty-three miles of Lake George. This was a bad start.

With Schuyler's aid Knox had arranged to have forty-two strong sleds built and eighty yoke of oxen and horses, mostly oxen, assembled at or near Fort George. From there, December 17, he wrote to Washington: "I hope in 16 or 17 days' time to be able to present to your Excellency a noble train of artillery."

But—he could not go until there was snow. He chafed.

He had planned his route to be down the west bank of the Hudson as far as Albany, then to cross the river and down the east bank as far as Kinderhook, from whence to turn due east across the Berkshires, through Great Barrington, Monterey, Otis, Blandford, Westfield, Springfield, and so to Cambridge. A forethinking man, he had written to the committees of safety of all these towns, announcing his imminent arrival and begging that they provide fodder for the beasts, food and drink for the men, shelter for both.

He also wrote, from Fort George, to the man he had treated with in New York, Colonel Alexander MacDougal, suggesting that if MacDougal could find any he might send some 13-inch mortar shells to the camp at Cambridge. Those three mortars had been an unexpected find at Ticonderoga, and Henry Knox did not want to see them wasted. He did not know—he could not know then—that the Continental Army had recently acquired another such piece, the one from the *Nancy*, the one that Old Put had christened with a bottle of rum.

At last, on Christmas Eve, it began blessedly to snow. They pushed off.

# CHAPTER

# 29

It was bitterly cold, and the fight against frozen feet and frozen fingers was a large part of their work at first.

Glens Falls was the first town they came upon, and their presence there created a sensation, people gawping. Knox, on a horse at the head of the advance party, would occasionally ride back along the whole line, shouting orders where needed: he had a deep strong voice, the voice of a clipper skipper in a gale. He was conscious of the figure he cut and not displeased by it.

They had prayed for snow, but when it came it came with too much gusto. On Christmas Day they were staggering through two feet of it, and the stuff still was falling. The advance party borrowed a sleigh and hitched their horses to that, but the great majority of the men, countrymen and soldiers lent by Schuyler, had to slog along on foot. The oxen were better at this sort of thing than were the horses, but Knox could seldom get as many oxen as he wanted. For all the "spare no expense" clause in his orders, he was limited to twelve shillings a pair a day, and in the case of the horses— plow horses, of course—he sometimes had to do a great deal of old-fashioned Yankee bargaining, plus not a little rhetorical appeal to patriotism, to get even these terms. He was quite capable of this.

He was not as harsh a haggler, however, as the wealthy Philip Schuyler, to whom he now, in advance of the heavy guns, appealed for further help. Drivers' wages and the hire of horses and oxen had gone up suddenly, the General noted, and he did not like it. For four days he did the best he could, and eventually he got a good supply of additional sleds and beasts to pull and men to maintain and repair them. These two, Schuyler and Knox, were about to sit down to a dinner to celebrate the exploit when Knox was notified that in an attempt to cross the Mohawk at Lansing's Ferry the men had lost a big gun, an 18-pounder, which crashed through the ice. Nothing else had been lost. Knox hurried to the scene and supervised the rescue work. Fortunately the water was shallow at this point, near where the Mohawk empties into the Hudson, and they soon had the big weapon to the surface again. They moved then a little upriver to Klaus's Ferry, where they crossed. It was a ticklish business, for the ice was thin, but they made it, all but one small cannon, which they abandoned at the bottom of the river.[55]

January 4, they began reeling into Albany well behind schedule. There another shock awaited them—a thaw. The river could not be crossed on foot just then, yet it was too crammed with ice floes to be crossed in boats. All that they could do was wait; and they waited two days.

Once again, when at last they made the crossing, they were to lose a gun through the ice, another big one—it made an eighteen-foot hole—despite extensive precautions. The water was not deep, however, and here they had any amount of civilian assistance, for the artillery train had caused a stir in Albany, which regarded it as a sort of municipal obligation. The cannon was rescued, and as a means of thanks for the help of the townspeople it was, there and then, christened the Albany.

Now they were on the east bank, and well away from the difficult foothills of the Adirondacks. The train was not one glorious column but a strung-out affair of fits and starts. At certain points like Albany a wait would be made for the stragglers, but in the open country between stops each section struggled along as best as it could, and if one sled in it broke down the whole section went to work on it until it was prepared to go forward again. The largest section was made up of fourteen sleds. Some were drawn by two horses or oxen, some by four or six, a few by eight. They used to get started before sunrise every morning.

They took the Old Post Road to Kinderhook and then went south to Claverack, where a broken sled held them up for two days.

Every town and village they passed through received them tumultuously. Most of the men and women who crowded around to stare—and to offer food and drink—had never before seen any kind of cannon, much less such huge ones. It was a sight that they would never forget. It was also, incidentally, a boost for the Continental cause.

At Hillsdale they turned sharply east, crossed the Massachusetts–New York line, and met the Berkshires head on. In summer these are pretty little hills; but in winter they can be decidedly grim. This—and they had known that it would be—was the hardest part of the trek. Often they could not even find any semblance of a road,[56] and there was at least one time when the men refused to tackle such terrible steeps and such high passes, and Knox had to argue with them for three hours, promising all sorts of impromptu safety devices, before they would consent to give it another try.

There was one stretch of almost forty miles in which they passed not even the smallest farmhouse or barn.

At Westfield they knew that the worst was behind them, and they relaxed a little, this process being made the easier by reason of the generosity of the inhabitants, who kept bringing out all sorts of drinks. To say thanks for such hospitality they forgot the shortage of gunpowder for the moment and loaded one of the heaviest and fattest of the brass 13-inchers, one they affectionately called the Old Sow, and fired it. Nobody there had ever before heard such a bang.

HENRY KNOX ENTERING CAMP WITH THE ARTILLERY
FROM FORT TICONDEROGA

Once they were out of the hills the snow became less co-operative, and there were even some bare patches. At Springfield the New York men, the civilians, balked. There was a tremendous thaw on, and they could not possibly continue, they said, unless other arrangements were made—meaning wagons—or unless it began to freeze and to snow all over again. They had been away for a long while, and they wanted to go home. Knox did not dicker with them, but paid them off. The guns were half sunk into mud by the side of the road, but he knew now that he could get local men or soldiers, or both, to finish the job.

This he did, and in a few days the guns were moved on as far as Framingham. There Henry Knox left them and rode on ahead to report, January 24, to his Commander-in-Chief in Cambridge.

It had taken him somewhat longer than he, in his inexperience, had predicted; but he had done the work, and George Washington congratulated him.

# 30

GUNPOWDER was trickling in. It came from France and Spain and the Netherlands, mostly by way of the tiny Dutch West Indies island of St. Eustatius; but some was captured by privateers, while a little too was manufactured at home.

Washington had the heaviest pieces from Ticonderoga posted at Lechmere Point, at Cobble Hill, and at Roxbury, and the night of Saturday, March 2, these opened on the town of Boston, the first time the Americans had really spoken in an unmistakable voice, the voice of the big guns. The bombardment was promptly answered by the British in redoubled and quadrupled form; but the Americans *had* spoken, and it was always good to know that you had a lot of noise on your side.

Neither did any notable harm. But—why were the rebels using all that powder? It looked like a softening-up process. Howe's observation officers at Boston Neck and on Bunker Hill were especially attentive with their glasses Sunday morning.

Those on the hill saw many signs of approaching battle. Supplies were being moved. Preparations were being made for the taking away of the wounded. This, then, was the direction from which the attack would come? Very well.

The artillery duel was resumed that night, Sunday, and again on Monday night. It was so thorough that it dried up many of the wells in the vicinity.

All this while, hidden from the sight of the British by the hills of Dorchester Neck, Washington was assembling men and oxen and guns for the fortification of those very hills. The preparations to the north were no more than a feint.

On the Monday night hundreds of oxen patiently plodded up the heights of Dorchester, hauling all manner of fascines and chandeliers and gabions, also scores of barrels which were to be filled with dirt and stones and rolled down upon the British if the British decided to dispute the occupation of *this* peninsula as well.

An east wind helped, so that the occupiers of Boston did not hear a sound.

The next morning—it was the sixth anniversary of the Boston Massacre—the Continentals were seen to have two full-fledged forts and four fortified positions in Dorchester. Undoubtedly they were the greatest diggers in the world. Here was a masterwork of defense construction. General Howe, studying it through a glass, estimated that it must have taken at least 12,000 men to build (actually it had taken about 2,000). Howe, after consultation with the new admiral, Molyneau Shuldham, decided that he could not tolerate it. The thing must go. He ordered a bombardment of the new rebel position.

It was no use. All the cannons in Boston blasted away for two hours, but they could not elevate their muzzles enough to reach the positions on Dorchester.

On the other hand, the rebels had not yet been able to seize the prize position of all, Nook's Hill, the highest place on the peninsula and the nearest to Boston. If they ever got into position there with their new-found cannons they would control not only the whole city but the whole bay and Fort William beyond.

Howe ordered an attack. He started shifting men across the bay to Fort William, obviously with the idea of making a massive landing on the east side of the peninsula of Dorchester. The guns had not been emplaced in the American fortifications, nor the breastworks built, with an attack from that quarter in mind. There were frantic changes, a welter of work.

Providence interceded, or so said the pious Massachusetts men; and it certainly did look like that. The wind, which had been so accommodating the first night the trenches were dug, suddenly and unaccountably swerved to the west, and at the same time it grew cold and wet, the air flecked with face-stinging rain.

Howe waited through three days of this unprecedented weather. He could not, in all humanity, launch an attack against such a wind—almost a hurricane. His men would be worn out before they even got to Dorchester. And he was not likely to forget Breed's Hill.

At last he gave up, and returned his men to Boston; and the wind immediately slacked off.

Yes, unquestionably God was on the side of the rebels.

The night of March 16 Washington took and emphatically fortified Nook's Hill itself; and then it was all over.

The generals must have had some manner of communicating with each other, though neither of them would admit it, for it was perfectly understood that if Washington bombarded Boston from the heights of Dorchester the British would burn the city. On the other hand, if Washington refrained from bombardment the British would get out. This was as plain on both sides as though it had been in writing.

The British did just that. They lived up to their word. March 17—the day has been celebrated in Boston ever since, though not always for the same reason—they evacuated Boston. They blew up magazines of ammunition and supplies, they spiked more then two hundred cannons, and escorted more than 1,100 Loyalists, plus 667 female camp followers, aboard of the 170 vessels in the bay. Howe's own forces, numbering then about 14,500 men, were also put aboard. It was a brilliantly executed retreat.

The officer in charge of the evacuation of Charlestown

Peninsula managed to hold off an American attack by the ingenious use of straw men dressed in British uniforms and stationed at the points where ordinarily British sentinels *had* been stationed. One of these bore a sign around its neck: "Yankees, good bye!"

For reasons best known to themselves—there must after all have been a great deal of straightening-out to do—the British lay in the bay for ten days; but on March 27 they sailed out to sea, a mighty if motley fleet, an armada. "They look like a forest," Abigail Adams told her husband in a letter.[57]

Henry Knox put in a bill for all expenses of £521 15s 8 3/4d. It was not much to pay for a city the size of Boston.

# NOTES

1. Barker, *Diary*.
2. De Bernière, *Narrative*.
3. Even making allowance for poetic license, Longfellow was hilariously inaccurate when he wrote the *Innkeeper's Story* in his *Tales of a Wayside Inn*. Thus:

> "One, if by land, and two, if by sea;"

But the old Back Bay and the shallow mouth of the Charles made up an odd "sea."

> "I on the opposite shore will be,"

But Revere was in midstream when the lanterns were put into place, an act with which he had nothing to do, for they were not meant for him but for Colonel Conant at Charlestown.

> "To the highest window in the wall,"

But there were only two windows in the steeple of the Old North Church.

> "It was one by the village clock,
> "When he galloped into Lexington."

But there was no village clock; and he got there a little after twelve.

> "It was two by the village clock,
> "When he came to the bridge in Concord town,"

But there were in fact two bridges, and he would have had to pass clear through the center of town and beyond to get to either of them; and anyhow, he never did reach Concord that morning.

> "To every Middlesex village and farm,—"

Granted that he did a good job, he probably did not reach a tenth of the farms and villages in Middlesex County. The system was, generally, that Revere would wake up the local militia leader, who then would spread the alarm among his men.

Where Longfellow was smart, or perhaps just lucky, was in that he did not attribute the lantern-hanging to anybody more definite than "a friend," and thus took no sides in the controversy that was to rage for years between the believers in Robert Newman, the North Church sexton, and the patriot Captain John Pulling, Jr., a deacon. North Church, parenthetically, was not the real name of the structure, only the nickname. The real name was Christ Church, and it was Episcopalian.

4. Revere to Dr. Jeremy Belknap, Proceedings of the Massachusetts Historical Society, XVI, November, 1878, pp. 371–76.

5. Menotomy is now called West Cambridge. At one time, too, it was called Arlington.

6. Dawes had started about an hour earlier than Revere, but he had ridden farther. He had done more door-knocking, too. A historian of a later generation, Frank Coburn (see BIBLIOGRAPHY), in 1911, before every last vestige of the old landmarks had disappeared, rode over both routes on a bicycle, to which he had attached a cyclometer. He reported that Revere had covered 12 86/88ths miles, Dawes 16 61/88ths miles. Actually, Dr. Prescott, who was to keep busy for the rest of the night, may have ridden farther and carried the message to more men than either of the others.

7. Dr. Prescott never did get the girl. He was to die in 1777, a surgeon in the Continental Army, as a prisoner of war in Halifax. Lydia married somebody else and moved out of town.

8. He was to become a Signer, and, after the war, governor of Massachusetts. It was in this latter capacity that

he supervised the redistricting of the state in such a way that his own party was sure of election. This involved some tortuous cartographical convolutions, and a friend, studying a map of one of the most notably misshapen voting districts, observed that it looked like a salamander. "Say rather a *gerry*mander," somebody else remarked; and a useful word was added to the American language.

9. Deserters from the British Army were exceedingly welcome in small Massachusetts towns at that time, provided the towns were far enough from Boston for them to be safe from pursuit. Any regular private knew more than a provincial sergeant or even a captain about the "discipline," as the manual of arms was called. He would be well fed, treated like a human being. But the punishment, if he was caught and hauled back, was unspeakable.

10. He was the grandfather of Ralph Waldo Emerson, and lived in the Old Manse, the building a later occupant, Nathaniel Hawthorne, was to describe so feelingly.

11. These, together with the cartridges, weighed about 125 pounds. Stedman, I, 128; Curtis, 14–15.

12. One of their favorite songs, "Yankee Doodle," was written originally in derision of the goggle-eyed hayseed who gawps at a proper army encampment inhabited largely by brightly dressed illiterates, and it still had this meaning at the beginning of the Revolution, though the Continentals were to twist it into a defiant air of cheer and triumph. The derivation of "Yankee" is in doubt, though not because of a lack of theories, perhaps the best of which is that it was a smearing together of Jan (pronounced "Yahn") and Kees, which is to say, in Dutch, John Cheese, a name the original settlers of New Amsterdam sometimes bestowed, disparagingly, upon their neighbors to the east. This is the theory favored by the *Oxford Dictionary*, the *Dictionary of American English*, the late H. L. Mencken (*The American Language*, Supplement I, 192–97), and the late Oscar George

Theodore Sonneck (*Report on 'The Star-Spangled Banner,'* *'Hail Columbia,' 'America,' 'Yankee Doodle'* [Washington: U.S. Government Printing Office, 1909]). As for "doodle," Dr. Johnson in his dictionary calls this a contraction of "do" and "little," but he was just guessing. The word was popular well before his time, Noodle and Doodle being clowns in many a Restoration comedy, brainless buffoons, they who get slapped. The word could, of course, be onomatopoeic.

13. The dispute was to last for years, to no purpose. It could have been ended when Benjamin Franklin quietly asked, after an English friend had been spluttering about the barbarity of firing from behind walls, "Weren't there two sides to those walls?"

14. It and the saddle were sold next day at auction, and the proceeds went to the Cause. A couple of fine pistols were holstered on the saddle, and these were presented to the Connecticut hero Israel Putnam, who carried them throughout the war: you can see them today in the museum at Lexington.

15. They lost two men in the afternoon conflict, old Jedediah Munroe, who had survived the morning massacre, and young Jack Raymond, who had not been there, having overslept.

16. Mackenzie, *Diary*, I, 21–2.

17. You may see his home in Shrewsbury, a public shrine; but it is a shrine not often visited, for the average American has never even heard of Artemas Ward. There are sundry reasons for this. For one thing, until a few years ago there was no published life of Ward, though this has been changed by Martyn (see BIBLIOGRAPHY). For another, Ward's place was taken by a man who *did* catch the public's imagination, George Washington. Our grandparents were further confused by the fact that Artem*u*s Ward, so spelled, was the pen name of a *Cleveland Plain Dealer* writer, Charles Farrar Browne, whom for many years many thousands of

readers thought funny, though it is difficult to see, from this distance, why. Columnist Ward said that when he picked his pseudynom he had never heard of General Artem*a*s Ward. He didn't know where he got the name from—out of the nowhere.

18. It was to be better known in later years as the Holmes house, being the home of Oliver Wendell Holmes. It was torn down in 1884.

19. The figures are interesting. It might have been thought that there were scarcely 973 bayonets in the whole colony at that time, for the weapon was of no use against Indians. The number of pistols, too, startles. The pistol was an expensive and highly uncertain mechanism used by horsemen and duelists, but not often by army officers and almost never by civilians. As for blunderbusses, it is strange to see them in effect classed as military weapons. They never had any military value. The blunderbuss was a short musket with an enormous flaring muzzle. It could be loaded with stones, nails, almost anything, and would make a terrific explosion and spout a great deal of smoke, but it would carry only a few yards. The weapon was useful chiefly *ad terrorum*. It was favored by stagecoach drivers—but there were none such in America—and by householders who had some reason to fear burglars. Artists are fond of putting it into the hands of the original Pilgrim fathers, which is ridiculous: it would have been useless in the American wilderness.

20. Now Vermont. The territory was called that, though in fact New Hampshire had waived its claim a little while before. New York still claimed the territory, a claim the Green Mountain Boys rejected.

21. Several stands of colors were also presented to the Congress as souvenirs of victory, but Congress handled them gingerly at first, being somewhat afraid of them. At last, however, they were hung on the wall of the downstairs meeting room in the Pennsylvania State House (now Inde-

pendence Hall). You may see them in the background of John Trumbull's celebrated painting, *The Signing of the Declaration of Independence*.

22. Frothingham, *Siege*, 107.

23. *Letters*, 55.

24. French, *First Year*, 105-7; Curtis, *British Army*, 11 n.; Blumenthal, *passim*.

25. This organization still exists. In its colonial uniforms, and with its muskets, it marches at inaugurals and other momentous occasions.

26. "He is the toast of the army," Silas Dean wrote. "He does not wear a large wig, nor screw his countenance into a form that belies the sentiments of his generous soul; he is no adept either at politics or religious canting and cozening: he is no shake-hand body: he therefore is totally unfit for everything but fighting." *Papers*, I, 74.

27. *Letters*, 64.

28. "He [Prescott] had literally thrust his head into the Lion's mouth," Charles Francis Adams was to write (*Studies*, 3) with a fine disregard for the fauna of eastern Massachusetts.

29. He was later to organize a company of rangers for irregular warfare, and in this capacity he was to give a spying assignment to one of his most promising subalterns, the schoolteacher Nathan Hale. Soon after the execution of Hale, Knowlton himself was killed at the battle of Harlem Heights.

30. Frothingham, *Siege*, 116-7.

31. *Letters*, 52.

32. Abigail Adams: "Courage I know we have in abundance; conduct I hope we shall not want; but powder,— where shall we get a sufficient supply?" *Letters*, 63.

33. The word means "arrows" in French.

34. Heath, *Memoirs*, 123.

35. *The Oxford Dictionary of Quotations* (2nd edition) credits Israel Putnam with this, but it is not likely.

Putnam did get around a great deal that day, but when the British were approaching he was almost certainly on Bunker's Hill. Bartlett attributes the command to William Prescott. Fleming (*Story of Bunker Hill*, 237) and Bartlett say (though without citing an authority) that the whites-of-their-eyes command was originated by Prince Charles of Prussia in the Battle of Jägerndorf, in 1745.

36. Taking part on the British side were the flank companies alone of the 4th, 10th, 18th, 22nd, 23rd, 35th, 59th, 63rd, and 65th infantry regiments, together with the whole strength of the 5th, 38th, 43rd, 47th, and 52nd, and two weak battalions of marines. Sir John Fortescue (*British Army*, III, 159 n.) has found that by error the wounded of the 38th were not counted in the official report. The number will never be known, but since that regiment suffered the largest number killed—25—Sir John reckons that its wounded must have amounted to "at least 100," which would bring the total British casualties to 1,150.

37. They were to lose more men by surrender at Saratoga and at Yorktown, but in killed and wounded Bunker's Hill was for the British by far the costliest battle of the whole eight years of the American Revolution.

38. Here are thoughts on that matter by two distinguished military historians, one American, the other English:

"The practical effect of Bunker Hill on the course of the siege of Boston, and of the whole Revolution, was to encourage a false belief in the people-in-arms, and the confidence that at any crisis the swarming of the militia to the field would meet all emergencies. The result was a weakening of the army, and the coming of crises which need never have risen." French, *First Year*, 267.

"For the rest, the combat produced a remarkable effect on the future operations of the war. It shook the nerve of Howe, and showed the British that the subjugation of the Colonies would be no child's-play. On the other hand, it not only elated the Americans, as was but natural and just, but encouraged them to a blind and fatal confidence in undisciplined troops, which went near to bring ruin to their cause. Notwithstanding the mistakes of generals and the deplorable waste of excellent troops, Bunker's Hill was probably a greater misfortune, taken altogether, to the Americans than to the British." Fortescue, *British Army*, III, 162.

39. *Writings*, III, 309.

40. *Writings*, III, 440.

41. It is notable that though the Commander-in-Chief felt called upon to issue an order forbidding "playing at Cards, and other Games of Chance" (*Writings*, IV, 347) in the camp, one of the most popular gambling games of the late eighteenth and early nineteenth centuries was named Boston, after the siege, not the city. This was a modification of whist, ancestor of our current contract bridge, and it appears to have been invented by officers on a French warship anchored near the end of the Revolution off Marblehead, Massachusetts, two of its terms, Great Misery and Little Misery, being named after islands there. Anything to do with Boston was popular at the time in France, where American visitors were hailed as Bostonians. The game was always more popular there. Benjamin Franklin was said to have been expert at it. New Orleans, with its heavy French population, early developed a Boston Club, which still exists: it is named after the game, not the city.

42. The name is believed to have originated in Deuteronomy 25:3 or II Corinthians 11:23. It was a common expression, on sea as on land, and in general was considered a mild punishment. Washington in time was to be obliged to step up the lashings and extend them sometimes to as many as 100 strokes—in the British Army 1,000 was not uncommon—but at Cambridge Moses' Law was the limit.

43. *Writings*, III, 433.

44. *Writings*, IV, 124.

45. It is even asserted by some authorities that the principle of rifling antedated the invention of the gun itself, for the feathering on crossbow quarrels was slanted in such a way as to give those quarrels when fired a decided spin.

46. Frothingham, *Siege*, 228.

47. Charles Lee, the lanky second-in-command, at the same time had moved to General Royall's house in Medford, which with characteristic playfulness he named Hobgoblin Hall, so that President Langdon, who lived alone, had the big house on Cambridge Common all to himself again.

48. You can see that letter today at the Library of Congress.

49. Force, 4 *Annals*, III, 1479–86.

50. Connecticut was a sort of American Siberia, a suitable place to which to exile troublesome Tories. William Franklin, Benjamin's illegitimate son, and the deposed governor of New Jersey, for instance, was sent there for the duration. So was the Reverend (later Bishop) Samuel Seabury. After the British got out of Boston, Dr. Church was allowed to return to his home, where he was kept under a species of house arrest until late in 1777 when he asked for and was granted permission to make a trip to the West Indies. The vessel on which he sailed was never seen again. See French, *General Gage's Informers;* Van Doren, *Secret History*, etc. The only thing against Church, really, was that one weird letter, and until lately he still had a few half-hearted defenders; but the opening up of Gage's private correspondence proved his guilt beyond a doubt. He was the first American traitor. The British government granted his widow an allowance.

51. William was nineteen at the time. These two were all that was left of ten sons. Henry was the seventh, William the youngest. With two others they were the only ones to survive into maturity, and the two others, both older, had failed to return from a voyage to the West Indies, something that had happened also to their father, though not at the same

time. To Henry, twelve at the time, had been left the entire support of his mother and his younger brother; and that was when he had to drop out of school. He was always very close to William, and saw to it that the boy got a much better *formal* education than he, Henry, could have afforded. See the biographies of Henry Knox—Brooks, Drake, and Callahan—in the SELECTED BIBLIOGRAPHY.

52. The present town of Lake George. There was not even a village there at the time, only a fort.

53. Tradition has it that in the course of this journey to Ticonderoga they slept one night in a hut in the company of a south-bound prisoner of war on parole, a young British Army lieutenant named John André. But then, tradition has a lot of things that need hardly give historians pause; and in this case tradition could scarcely be expected to ignore the enticing fact that years later Brigadier General Knox was to be a member of the court-martial that sentenced Major André to be hanged as a spy. It *could* have happened; but there is no proof that it did. The night of December 5–6 is the one usually assigned to this momentous meeting, though from his letters and diary alike it is almost certain that Henry Knox spent that night at Ticonderoga, where even then accommodations were such that he would hardly be housed in a one-room hut. The story seems to have stemmed wholly from Thacher, a dubious authority who did not even pretend to have it first-hand. Even Thacher says only that the two men spent the night in the same building. All the rest—the two sitting up by the fire all night, fascinated by each other, the heartfelt handshake of farewell the next morning, Knox's unwillingness to look the prisoner in the face at the time of the court-martial, etc.—is embroidery.

54. Authorities differ on the actual number of pieces Knox picked for transportation, ranging all the way from 55 to 78. I have relied upon Flick, who publishes Knox's own inventory in full. *Expedition*, 124–25.

The reader at this point might well ask: *Why*, if it had

been possible to assemble such a great number of heavy guns in so remote a place, should it be so difficult to get them away again? There are several parts to the answer. In the first place the cannon had been carried there over a period of years by two world powers equipped with professional armies, not by a weak emergent nation with no full-time professional equipment and which aspired to do the job in a few weeks. In the second place, most or all of them undoubtedly had been brought there in the summer; whereas Knox necessarily was operating in the middle of winter, a rough season in those parts. But the most important thing to remember is that because of sea power the guns either had been floated up the Hudson and hauled across to Fort George and then floated to Ticonderoga, or else, more often, they had been floated up the St. Lawrence and up the Richelieu to a point from where it was only a short portage to the upper end of Lake Champlain. More than nine-tenths of Knox's route was to be overland.

55. It was hauled out, much later, and you may see it today in the museum that is Fort Ticonderoga.

56. The present Route 23.

57. *Familiar Letters*, 142.

# GLOSSARY OF EIGHTEENTH-CENTURY MILITARY TERMS

ABATIS. Chopped-down trees piled one on top of another, with the branches, sharpened, pointing toward an expected enemy. It serves, among other things, as a roadblock.

BARBETTE. A wooden or earthen platform, inside a fortification, on which cannons were placed in order to allow them to shoot over the rampart; a firing step.

BASTION. A projecting masonry work, usually V-shaped, on the wall of a fort, outside. From it, attackers along the CURTAIN could be cross-fired upon.

BLUNDERBUSS. A short chunky weapon, a musket, featured by a huge bell-shaped muzzle. The blunderbuss could discharge a lethal shower of stones, nails, lead slugs, what-have-you—but only for a short distance. The popular picture has the Pilgrim Fathers carrying blunderbusses, but it is hard to see why they should. The blunderbuss was no good as a bird gun, and any reasonably nimble Indian could hurl his tomahawk four times the distance that a blunderbuss would carry. The blunderbuss was never, properly, a military weapon. It was favored by stagecoach drivers and by householders who had some reason to fear burglars.

BROWN BESS. The nickname of a musket introduced into the British Army in 1682 and which, with minor modifications, continued to be the official infantry arm until 1842. It was, for the time, unexpectedly short and light; and it was efficient. That it was not accurate did not trouble military men, who placed all emphasis on controlled mass firepower rather than upon marksmanship. It could be reloaded very quickly. Americans treasured the Brown Bess muskets whenever they could get them from prisoners or corpses. The gun had a naturally brown walnut stock, while its barrel and other metal parts had been artificially browned with an antirust acid: hence the name.

CANISTER. A canvas or cloth bag filled with small round lead or iron pellets and crammed into a cannon on top of a charge of gunpowder. It would not carry as far as solid shot, but it was deadly at close quarters.

CARCASS. Nothing to do with a cadaver. It was a metal can punched with holes and filled with oiled rags that were set ablaze when the carcass was shot from a cannon. The purpose, of course, was to cause a building or a whole town to catch fire. Though still in an experimental stage, it was much favored at this time by the navy.

CASE SHOT. Another name for CANISTER.

CHEVAUX-DE-FRISE. A crisscross of heavy timbers, usually tipped with metal spikes, calculated to stop infantry.

CHANDELIERS. These did not look anything like the object the word ordinarily brings to mind. They were wooden frames, square or rectangular, which were filled with FASCINES in order to protect men who were digging entrenchments. Many chandeliers were used in the fortification of Dorchester Neck.

COHORN. This is one of the few words in the military vocabulary of the time that was not French. It was a small stubby MORTAR, and the name is an Anglification of that of the Dutch inventor Baron Coehoorn.

COUNTERSCARP. The outer wall or slope of the ditch surrounding a fort. The inner wall, usually higher, was the SCARP.

COVERED WAY. A roofed firing step to protect the protectors of the COUNTERSCARP.

CROW'S-FEET. Steel or iron spikes spreading out from a center in such a way that, no matter how they were thrown, at least one spike of each always pointed up. They were much used against cavalry.

CURTAIN. The wall of a fortification between towers or other projections.

DEMILUNE. A half-moon-shaped outwork, never large.

EMBRASURE. An opening in a PARAPET through which a cannon is fired.

ÉPAULEMENT. The "shoulder" of a fort wall; the place where the CURTAIN and the BASTION meet.

FASCINE. A bundle of twigs and sticks hastily assembled and tied together. They were used for constructing gun platforms and for filling ditches to permit the passage of military vehicles. From such a bundle, the symbol of ancient Rome, came the name of the late unlamented Fascists.

FEU DE JOIE. A musket salute performed by two double files, every other man firing the first time, the rest the second time coming back. A complicated business, it was reserved for special occasions. It was not often practiced in the Continental Army, which did not have the powder to spare.

FLANK COMPANIES. In each British infantry regiment there were a company of grenadiers and a company of so-called light infantry, and these were traditionally placed upon the flanks. They were elite troops.

FLASH-IN-THE-PAN. When, as so often happened, the tricker was pulled and the striker fell upon the flint, it produced sparks but not sufficient fire to cause an explosion; this was known as a flash-in-the-pan, the pan in question being the firing pan. This did not mean that the musket or pistol had to be reloaded, only that it had to be reprimed.

FLÈCHE. A small defensive ditch, unroofed, in the shape of an arrowhead (the word means "arrow" in French), the point toward the expected enemy. It was an outwork, a deterrent, a stopgap, not a real fortlet.

FRIZZEN. The steel cover of the priming pan, against the inside of which—when it was open—the striker slammed its chip of flint, causing a shower of sparks down into the pan.

GABIONS. These were baskets made of any available material, wicker being preferred, and filled with earth and stones. Clumsy, heavy things, they were used for shoring up parapets, filling ditches, protecting field guns: they were, in short, the eighteenth-century equivalent of sandbags.

GLACIS. The place between the natural level of the ground and the covered way, artificially sloped so that every part of it can be covered by fire from the parapets.

GRAPE or GRAPESHOT. Similar to CANISTER except that the balls were smaller and there were more of them.

HOWITZER. A term that meant then exactly what it does today—a smallish cannon sharply uptilted, used, mostly in mountain warfare, to lob shells or balls into a protected position.

MATROSS. A sort of assistant artilleryman who helped to handle a fieldpiece in action. He was a regular member of the army, not like the civilian horse drivers who retired when the guns began to boom—if not before.

MORTAR. Just what it is now—a short large-calibered piece of ordnance so trunnioned that it can shoot very high.

PARAPET. The wall of a fortification.

PICKET, sometimes PIQUET. A small party of foot soldiers sent forth in advance of the army to feel out the enemy and harass him if he approaches.

POUNDAGE. Field guns, whether on ship or ashore, were rated by the weight of the balls they could fire, which weight was reckoned in pounds avoirdupois. Thus, 4-pounder, 6-pounder, etc. A 3-pounder was very small, a 24-pounder very large. This applied only to solid shot, not to CANISTER or GRAPE or CARCASSES.

RAMPART. Parapet.

RAVELIN. This was a small earthwork, an outwork, with only two faces, something like a FLÈCHE.

REDAN. It would take an expert to distinguish this from a RAVELIN, though it might be somewhat smaller.

REDOUBT. This was larger and stronger than a RAVELIN or a REDAN. It might be square or some other multiangled shape, but it was always completely enclosed, never open at one end. The first fortification on Breed's Hill, the American one, was commonly called a redoubt, though properly it was not, being open in back.

SAUCISSON. This, in French, means a large or German-type sausage. In eighteenth-century armies it meant a large FASCINE of roughly that shape.

SNAPHAUNCE or SNAPHANCE. This is another of the rare non-French military terms of the time. It means, in Dutch, "pecking hen," a reference to its action when the striker was released.

The snaphaunce was the earliest form of spring trigger action, succeeding the matchlock and the expensive wheel lock.

SPONTOON. This was a sort of halberd or pike carried by sergeants on both sides, for protection, when battle was expected. Often, too, they were carried by officers, whose toothpicky swords were largely ornamental, symbolic.

TENAILLE. A small, low fortification, sometimes with only one entrance, sometimes with two, occasionally roofed, placed for annoyance purposes outside the CURTAIN between two BASTIONS.

UP IN THE AIR. An unprotected flank, such as the Continental left on Long Island, was said to have been left "up in the air."

VAUBAN SYSTEM. Sébastien le Prestre de Vauban was history's greatest military engineer. Born poor, he died a Marshal of France. As soon as he had built an impregnable fort, he would proceed to devise a way to take it; and then, when he built his next fort, he would allow for this. Thus, the phrase "Vauban system" applies to both defensive and offensive fortification warfare. Developed in the latter part of the seventeenth century, it was standard practice for all Western military men throughout the eighteenth and nineteenth centuries; it was still in effect in various places as late as the beginning of World War I.

# SELECTED BIBLIOGRAPHY

ADAIR, DOUGLASS, see OLIVER, PETER.

ADAMS, ABIGAIL, see ADAMS, CHARLES FRANCIS.

ADAMS, CHARLES FRANCIS. "The Battle of Bunker Hill from a Strategic Point of View." Proceedings of the American Antiquarian Society, New Series, X, Worcester, Mass., 1896.
———, editor. *Familiar Letters of John Adams and His Wife Abigail Adams During the Revolution.* New York: Hurd and Houghton, 1876.
———, *Studies Military and Diplomatic.* New York: The Macmillan Company, 1911.
———, editor. *The Works of John Adams, With Life.* 10 vols. Boston: Little, Brown and Company, 1850–56.

ADAMS, JAMES TRUSLOW. *Revolutionary New England, 1691–1776.* Boston: Little, Brown and Company, 1927.

ADAMS, JOHN, see ADAMS, CHARLES FRANCIS.

ALDEN, JOHN RICHARD. *The American Revolution, 1775–1783.* New York: Harper & Brothers, 1954.
———. *General Gage in America, Being Principally a History of His Role in the American Revolution.* Baton Rouge: Louisiana State University Press, 1948.
———. "Why the March to Concord?" *The American Historical Review,* XLIX, 446–54.

ALLEN, PAUL. *A History of the American Revolution.* Baltimore: Franklin Betts, 1822.

ANDERSON, TROYER STEELE. *The Command of the Howe Brothers During the American Revolution.* New York and London: Oxford University Press, 1936.

ANDREWS, CHARLES M. *The Colonial Background of the American Revolution.* New Haven: Yale University Press, 1924.

BAKER, WILLIAM SPOHN. *Itinerary of General Washington from June 15, 1775, to December 23, 1783.* Philadelphia: J. B. Lippincott Company, 1892.

BALDWIN, ALICE M. *The New England Clergy and the American Revolution.* Durham, N.C.: Duke University Press, 1928.

BANCROFT, GEORGE. *History of the United States of America,* 6 vols. New York: D. Appleton and Company, 1883.

BARKER, JOHN. *A British Officer in Boston in 1775.* Edited by R. H. Dana, Jr. *The Atlantic Monthly,* XXXIX, nos. CCXXXIV and CCXXXV, April and May 1877.
———. *The British in Boston, Being the Diary of Lieutenant John Barker of the King's Own Regiment From November 15, 1774, to May 31, 1776,* with notes by Elizabeth Ellery Dana. Cambridge: Harvard University Press, 1924.

BECKER, CARL. *The Eve of the Revolution: A Chronicle of the Breach With England.* New Haven: Yale University Press, 1918.

BELCHER, HENRY. *The First American Civil War,* 2 vols. London: Macmillan and Company, Ltd., 1911.

BLUMENTHAL, WALTER HART. *Women Camp Followers of the American Revolution.* Philadelphia: George S. McManus Company, 1952.

BOLTON, CHARLES KNOWLES, see also PERCY, HUGH EARL.
———. *The Private Soldier Under Washington.* New York: Charles Scribner's Sons, 1902.

BOTTA, CHARLES. *History of the War of Independence of the United States.* New Haven, Conn.: Whiting, 1837.

BRADFORD, ALDEN. *Complete and Authentic History of the Battle of Bunker Hill, June 17, 1775.* Boston: J. N. Bradley and Company, 1825.

BROOKS, NOAH. *Henry Knox, a Soldier of the Revolution.* New York: G. P. Putnam's Sons, 1900.

BROWN, MRS. REBECCA. *Stories About General Warren in Relation to the Fifth of March Massacre and the Battle of Bunker Hill.* Boston: James Loring, 1825.

BROWN, WELDON A. *Empire or Independence: A Study in the Failure of Reconciliation, 1774–1783.* Baton Rouge: Louisiana State University Press, 1941.

BURLEY, ANGELYN JEFFERDS. *General Artemas Ward: A Study.* Shrewsbury, Mass.: The General Artemas Ward Memorial Museum, 1950.

CALLAHAN, NORTH. *Henry Knox: General Washington's General.* New York: Rinehart & Company, Inc., 1958.

CARRINGTON, HENRY B. *Battles of the American Revolution: Historical and Military Criticism.* New York: A. S. Barnes & Company, 1876.

CARY, JOHN. *Joseph Warren: Physician, Politician, Patriot.* Urbana: University of Illinois Press, 1961.

CHANNING, EDWARD. *A History of the United States,* 6 vols. New York: The Macmillan Company, 1925.

CLARK, DORA MAE. *British Opinion and the American Revolution.* New Haven: Yale University Press, 1930.

CLARK, WILLIAM BELL. *George Washington's Navy.* Baton Rouge: Louisiana State University Press, 1960.

CLINTON, SIR HENRY. *The American Rebellion: Sir Henry Clinton's Narrative of His Campaigns, 1775–1782, With an Appendix of Original Documents,* edited by William B. Willcox. New Haven: Yale University Press, 1954.

COBURN, FRANK WARREN. *Battle of April 19th, 1775.* Lexington: privately printed, 1912.

COFFIN, CHARLES, editor. *History of the Battle of Breed's Hill, by Major-Generals William Heath, Charles Lee, James Wilkinson and Henry Dearborn.* Portland: D. C. Colesworthy, 1835.

COMMAGER, HENRY STEELE, and RICHARD B. MORRIS, *The Spirit of Seventy-Six: The Story of the American Revolution as Told by Participants.* Indianapolis and New York: The Bobbs-Merrill Company, Inc., 1958.

CURTIS, E. E. *The British Army in the American Revolution.* New Haven: Yale University Press, 1926.

DANA, E. E., see BARKER, JOHN.

DANA, R. H., JR., see BARKER, JOHN.

DAWSON, HENRY BARTON. *Battles of the United States, by Sea and Land,* 2 vols. New York: Johnson, Fry & Company, 1858.

DEANE, SILAS. *The Silas Deane Papers,* 5 vols. New York: Printed for the New-York Historical Society, 1887.

DEARBORN, HENRY. "Bunker's Hill." *Historical Magazine,* June 1868, 3., second series, No. 6, 321–440.

DE BERNIÈRE, HENRY. "Narrative of Occurrences, 1775." Massachusetts Historical Society Collections, second series, IV, 204.

DE FOREST, LOUIS E., see POMEROY, SETH.

DE PUY, HENRY W. *Ethan Allen and the Green-Mountain Boys.* Boston: Horace Wentworth, 1853.

DRAKE, FRANCIS SAMUEL. *Life and Correspondence of Henry Knox.* Boston: S. G. Drake, 1873.

DRAKE, SAMUEL ADAMS. *Bunker Hill: The Story Told in Letters From the Battle Field by British Officers Engaged.* Boston: Nichols & Hall, 1875.
———. *General Israel Putnam, the Commander at Bunker Hill.* Boston: Nichols & Hall, 1875.

ELLIS, G. EDWARD. *Sketches of Bunker Hill Battle and Monument, With Illustrative Documents.* 4th edition. Charlestown, Mass.: C. P. Emmons, 1844.

ESPOSITO, COLONEL VINCENT J., editor. *The West Point Atlas of American Wars.* New York: Frederick A. Praeger, 1959.

FALKNER, LEONARD. *Forge of Liberty*. New York: E. P. Dutton & Co., Inc., 1959.

FARNSWORTH, AMOS. "Diary." Proceedings of the Massachusetts Historical Society, XXXII: 79.

FISHER, SIDNEY GEORGE. "The Legendary and Myth-Making Process in Histories of the American Revolution." Proceedings of the American Philosophical Society, LI, No. 204, April–June, 1912.
———. *The Struggle for American Independence*, 2 vols. Philadelphia: J. B. Lippincott Company, 1909.

FISKE, JOHN. *The American Revolution*, 2 vols. Boston: Houghton Mifflin Company, 1891.

FITCH, JABEZ. "Diary." Proceedings of the Massachusetts Historical Society, XXXII: 29–40.

FITZPATRICK, JOHN CLEMENT, see WASHINGTON, GEORGE.

FLEMING, THOMAS J. *The Story of Bunker Hill*. New York: Collier Books, 1962.

FORBES, ESTHER. *Paul Revere and the World He Lived In*. Boston: Houghton Mifflin Company, 1942.

FORCE, PETER, editor. *American Archives*, 13 vols. Washington, D.C.: M. St. Clair Clarke and Peter Force, 1839.

FORTESCUE, JOHN W. *History of the British Army*, 10 vols. New York: The Macmillan Company, 1899–1920.

FREEMAN, DOUGLAS SOUTHALL. *George Washington: A Biography*, 6 vols. New York: Charles Scribner's Sons, 1948–1954.

FRENCH, ALLEN, see also MACKENZIE, FREDERICK.
———. *The Colonials, being a narrative of events chiefly connected with the siege and evacuation of the town of Boston in New England*. New York: Doubleday, Page, 1902.
———. *The Day of Concord and Lexington: The Nineteenth of April, 1775*. Boston: Little, Brown and Company, 1925.

————. *The First Year of the American Revolution*. Boston: Houghton Mifflin Company, 1934.

————. *General Gage's Informers: New Material Upon Lexington and Concord, Benjamin Thompson as Loyalist and the Treachery of Benjamin Church, Jr.* Ann Arbor: The University of Michigan Press, 1932.

————. *The Siege of Boston*. New York: The Macmillan Company, 1911.

————. *The Taking of Ticonderoga in 1775: The British Story*. Cambridge: Harvard University Press, 1928.

FROTHINGHAM, RICHARD. *History of the Siege of Boston and of the Battles of Lexington, Concord, and Bunker Hill*. Boston: Little, Brown and Company, 1872.

————. *Life and Times of Joseph Warren*. Boston: Little, Brown and Company, 1865.

————. "Remarks and Letters." Proceedings of the Massachusetts Historical Society, XIV: 261–98.

FULLER, J. F. C. *Decisive Battles of the U.S.A.* New York: Thomas Yoseloff, 1942.

GANOE, WILLIAM ADDLEMAN. *The History of the United States Army*. Revised edition. New York and London: D. Appleton-Century Company, 1943.

GIPSON, LAWRENCE HENRY. *The Coming of the American Revolution, 1763–1775*. New York: Harper & Brothers, 1954.

GORDON, WILLIAM. *The History of the Rise, Progress, and Establishment of the Independence of the United States of America*, 4 vols. London: Printed for the author, 1788.

HATCH, LOUIS CLINTON. *The Administration of the American Revolutionary Army*. New York: Longmans, Green & Co., 1904 (Harvard Historical Studies, X).

HEATH, WILLIAM. *Memoirs of Major-General Heath*. Boston: I. Thomas and E. T. Andrews, 1798.

HOLLAND, HENRY W. *William Dawes and His Ride with Paul Revere*. Boston: Privately printed, 1878.

How, David. *Diary*. Morrisania, N.Y.: Henry B. Dawson, 1865.

Hudson, Charles. "Life and Character of Major Pitcairn." Proceedings of the Massachusetts Historical Society, XVII, 1879–1880, 315–27.

Hudson, Frederic. "The Concord Fight." *Harper's New Monthly Magazine*, L, No. CCC, May 1875.

Hughes, Rupert. *George Washington*, 3 vols. New York: William Morrow & Company, 1927.

Humphreys, Col. David. *An Essay on the Life of the Honourable Major General Israel Putnam*, with an appendix on the Bunker Hill battle by S. Swett. Boston: Samuel Avery, 1818.

Hunt, Agnes. *The Provincial Committees of Safety of the American Revolution*. Cleveland: Western University Press, 1904.

Ketchum, Richard M. *The Battle for Bunker Hill*. Garden City: Doubleday & Company, 1962.

Knollenberg, Bernhard. "Bunker Hill Re-Viewed: A Study in the Conflict of Historical Evidence." Proceedings of the Massachusetts Historical Society, LXXII, 1963, 84–100.
———. *John Adams, Knox, and Washington*. Worcester, Mass.: American Antiquarian Society, 1947.
———. *Washington and the Revolution: A Reappraisal*. New York: The Macmillan Company, 1940.

Lecky, W. E. H. *History of England in the Eighteenth Century*, 8 vols. London: Longmans, Green & Co., 1878–1890.

Lister, Jeremy, see Murdock, Harold.

Lively, Robert A., see Wade, Herbert T.

Mackenzie, Frederick. *A British Fusilier in Revolutionary Boston, Being the Diary of Frederick Mackenzie*, edited by Allen French. Cambridge: Harvard University Press, 1926.

Martyn, Charles. *The Life of Artemas Ward, the First Commander-in-Chief of the American Revolution*. New York: Artemas Ward, 1921.

MELVIN, JAMES. *The Journal of James Melvin, Private Soldier in Arnold's Expedition Against Quebec.* Portland, Me.: Hubbard & Bryant, 1902.

MILLER, JOHN CHESTER. *Sam Adams, Pioneer in Propaganda.* Boston: Little, Brown and Company, 1936.

MONTRESOR, see SCULL, G. D.

MONTROSS, LYNN. *Rag, Tag and Bobtail: The Story of the Continental Army.* New York: Harper & Brothers, 1952.

MOORE, FRANK. *Songs and Ballads of the American Revolution.* New York: D. Appleton and Company, 1856.

MORGAN, EDMUND S. editor. *The American Revolution: Two Centuries of Interpretation.* Englewood Cliffs, N.J.: Prentice-Hall, Inc., 1965.

MORRIS, RICHARD B., see COMMAGER, HENRY STEELE.

MURDOCK, HAROLD. "The British at Concord—April 19, 1775." Proceedings of the Massachusetts Historical Society, LVI, November 1922, 70–94.
———. *Bunker Hill: Notes and Queries on a Famous Battle.* Boston: Houghton Mifflin Company, 1927.
———, editor. *Concord Fight: being so much of the Narrative of Ensign Jeremy Lister of the 10th Regiment of the Foot as Pertains to his Services on the 19th of April, 1775, and to his Experiences in Boston during the Early Months of the Siege.* Cambridge: Harvard University Press, 1931.
———. *Earl Percy's Dinner-Table.* Boston: Houghton Mifflin Company, 1907.
———. *The Nineteenth of April, 1775.* Boston: Houghton Mifflin Company, 1923.

MURRAY, SIR JAMES. *Letters From America, 1773 to 1780,* edited by Eric Robson. Manchester: Manchester University Press, 1951.

OLIVER, PETER, *Origin and Progress of the American Rebellion: A Tory View,* edited by Douglass Adair and John A. Schutz. San Marino, Calif.: The Huntington Library, 1961.

PARSONS, FRANCIS. "The British Attack on Bunker Hill." Paper read at a meeting of the Colonel Jeremiah Wadsworth Branch, Connecticut Society of the Sons of the American Revolution, Hartford Club, April 9, 1920.

PECKHAM, HOWARD H. *The War for Independence: A Military History*. Chicago: University of Chicago Press, 1958.

PERCY, HUGH EARL. *Letters of Hugh Earl Percy, From Boston and New York, 1774–1776*, edited by Charles Knowles Bolton. Boston: Charles E. Goodspeed, 1902.

PERRY, CLAY. "Big Guns for Washington." *American Heritage*, VI, No. 3, April 1955.

PHINNEY, ELIAS. *History of the Battle at Lexington*. Boston: 1825 and 1875.

POMEROY, SETH. *The Journals and Papers of Seth Pomeroy*, edited by Louis E. De Forest. New Haven, Conn.: Society of Colonial Wars in the State of New York, 1926.

POPE, RICHARD, see SUTHERLAND, LT. WILLIAM.

PRESCOTT, WILLIAM. "Account of the Battle of Bunker Hill." Proceedings of the Massachusetts Historical Society, XIV: 53.

PRICE, EZEKIEL. "Diary." Proceedings of the Massachusetts Historical Society, VII, 1863–4, 185–262.

PUTNAM, DANIEL. "Colonel Daniel Putnam's Letter Relative to the Battle of Bunker Hill and General Israel Putnam." Collections of the Connecticut Historical Society, I, Hartford, 1860.

REVERE, PAUL. "Letter to Dr. Jeremy Belknap." Proceedings of the Massachusetts Historical Society, XVI, 1878, 371–6.

REYNOLDS, REVEREND GRINDALL. *Historical and Other Papers*. Concord, 1896.

RIPLEY, EZRA. *A History of the Fight at Concord, on the 19th of April, 1775*. Concord, 1827.

ROBSON, ERIC, see also MURRAY, SIR JAMES.
———. *The American Revolution in Its Political and Military Aspects, 1763–1783.* London: The Batchworth Press, 1955.

SABINE, LORENZO. *Biographical Sketches of Loyalists of the American Revolution,* 2 vols. Boston: Little, Brown and Company, 1864.

SCHEER, GEORGE F. and HUGH F. RANKIN, *Rebels and Redcoats.* Cleveland and New York: The World Publishing Company, 1957.

SCHUTZ, JOHN A. see OLIVER, PETER.

SCULL, G. D., editor. *The Montresor Journals.* New York: The New-York Historical Society, 1881.

SHY, JOHN. *Toward Lexington: The Role of the British Army in the Coming of the American Revolution.* Princeton: Princeton University Press, 1965.

SMITH, JUSTIN H. *Our Struggle for the Fourteenth Colony: Canada and the American Revolution,* 2 vols. New York: G. P. Putnam's Sons, 1907.

STEDMAN, CHARLES. *The History of the Origin, Progress, and Termination of the American War,* 2 vols. London: Printed for the Author, 1794.

STORRS, EXPERIENCE. "Diary of Lieut. Col. Exp. Storrs, of Mansfield Cn." Proceedings of the Massachusetts Historical Society, XIV: 84–7; Magazine of American History, VIII, Part I, 124–7.

SUTHERLAND, LT. WILLIAM and RICHARD POPE. *Late News of the Excursions and Ravages of the King's Troops on the Nineteenth of April.* Cambridge: Harvard University Press, 1927.

SWETT, SAMUEL, see also HUMPHREYS, COL. DAVID.
———. *History of Bunker Hill Battle.* Boston: Monroe and Francis, 1827 (3rd edition).

TAYLOR, EMERSON. *Paul Revere.* New York: Edward Valentine and Dodd, Mead & Company, 1930.

TARBOX, INCREASE N. *Life of Israel Putnam* (*"Old Put"*). Boston: Lockwood, Brooks, and Co., 1876.

THACHER, JAMES. *Military Journal During the American Revolutionary War.* Boston: Richardson and Lord, 1823.

TOURTELLOT, ARTHUR BERNON. *William Diamond's Drum.* Garden City: Doubleday and Company, 1959.

TREVELYAN, GEORGE OTTO. *The American Revolution*, 6 vols. London: Longmans, Green & Company, 1905.

TYLER, MOSES COIT. *The Literary History of the American Revolution*, 2 vols. New York: G. P. Putnam's Sons, 1897.

VAN DOREN, CARL. *Secret History of the American Revolution.* New York: The Viking Press, 1941.

VAN TYNE, CLAUDE HALSTEAD. *The American Revolution.* New York: Harper & Brothers, 1905.
———. *England and America, Rivals in the American Revolution.* Cambridge: Cambridge University Press, 1929.
———. *The Loyalists in the American Revolution.* New York: Peter Smith, 1929.
———. *The War of Independence: American Phase.* Boston: Houghton Mifflin Company, 1929.

WADE, HERBERT T. and ROBERT A. LIVELY. *This Glorious Cause: The Adventures of Two Company Officers in Washington's Army.* Princeton: Princeton University Press, 1958.

WALLACE, WILLARD M. *Appeal to Arms: A Military History of the American Revolution.* New York: Harper & Brothers, 1951.

WARD, CHRISTOPHER. *The War of the Revolution*, 2 vols. New York: The Macmillan Company, 1952.

WASHINGTON, GEORGE. *The Writings of George Washington, From the Original Manuscript Sources, 1745–1799*, edited by John Clement Fitzpatrick, 39 vols. Washington: U.S. Government Printing Office, 1931–44.

WATSON, JOHN LEE. "Paul Revere's Signal: The True Story of the 'Signal Lanterns' in Christ Church, Boston." Proceedings of the Massachusetts Historical Society, XV, November 1876, 164–77.

WHARTON, FRANCIS, editor. *Revolutionary Correspondence of the United States*, 6 vols. Washington: U.S. Government Printing Office, 1889.

WHEELDON, WILLIAM W. *Siege and Evacuation of Boston and Charlestown*. Boston: Lee and Shepard, 1876.

WILLCOX, WILLIAM B., see CLINTON, SIR HENRY, also WYATT, FREDERICK.

WINSOR, JUSTIN. *The Memorial History of Boston*, 3 vols. Boston: J. R. Osgood and Co., 1880–81.

WYATT, FREDERICK, and WILLIAM B. WILLCOX. "Sir Henry Clinton: A Psychological Explanation in History." *The William and Mary Quarterly*, 3rd series, XVI, No. I, 3–26.

# Index

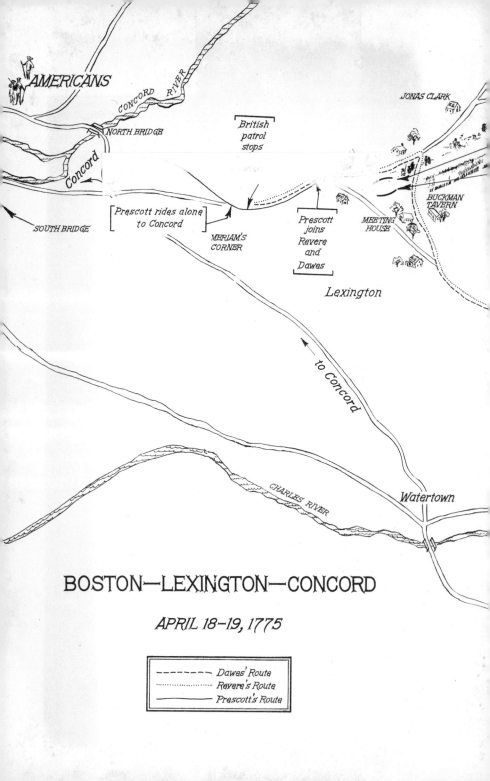

AMERICANS

CONCORD RIVER

NORTH BRIDGE

Concord

British
patrol
stops

JONAS CLARK

BUCKMAN
TAVERN

SOUTH BRIDGE

[ Prescott rides alone ]
to Concord

MERIAM'S
CORNER

Prescott
joins
Revere
and
Dawes

MEETING
HOUSE

Lexington

to Concord

CHARLES RIVER

Watertown

# BOSTON—LEXINGTON—CONCORD

## APRIL 18–19, 1775

––––––– Dawes' Route
················· Revere's Route
———— Prescott's Route